VICTIM
NO MORE!

How to Get Your Power Back

Jennifer Gamboa

BALBOA.
PRESS
A DIVISION OF HAY HOUSE

This book is a work of non-fiction. Unless otherwise noted, the author
and the publisher make no explicit guarantees as to the accuracy of
the information contained in this book and in some cases, names of
people and places have been altered to protect their privacy.

Balboa Press books may be ordered through booksellers or by contacting:

Balboa Press
A Division of Hay House
1663 Liberty Drive
Bloomington, IN 47403
www.balboapress.com
1 (877) 407-4847

Because of the dynamic nature of the Internet, any web addresses or
links contained in this book may have changed since publication and
may no longer be valid. The views expressed in this work are solely those
of the author and do not necessarily reflect the views of the publisher,
and the publisher hereby disclaims any responsibility for them.

The author of this book does not dispense medical advice or prescribe the use
of any technique as a form of treatment for physical, emotional, or medical
problems without the advice of a physician, either directly or indirectly. The
intent of the author is only to offer information of a general nature to help
you in your quest for emotional and spiritual well-being. In the event you use
any of the information in this book for yourself, which is your constitutional
right, the author and the publisher assume no responsibility for your actions.

Any people depicted in stock imagery provided by Getty Images are
models, and such images are being used for illustrative purposes only.
Certain stock imagery © Getty Images.

Print information available on the last page.

ISBN: 978-1-9822-1888-1 (sc)
ISBN: 978-1-9822-1886-7 (hc)
ISBN: 978-1-9822-1887-4 (e)

Library of Congress Control Number: 2018915031

Balboa Press rev. date: 05/10/2019

DEDICATION

This book is dedicated to the love of my life, my husband, Joseph Gamboa. He was my constant support system. He encouraged me to write this book.

My darling husband was my inspiration in life. He taught me how to seize life. He not only suggested I write a book, but he led by example and wrote a paperback full of knowledge and wit called, "When Trees Cry." As I edited his manuscript, I fell more in love with the man I planned to share my whole life in union with.

I would hear the pride in his voice and see the respect in his face for his father and his aunt "The Oracle" when he would share about his life. His father, his aunt, and his younger brother also were inspired by Joseph to write their books. Joseph was not the eldest son of his family, but he was the respected leader amassing success at the age of 36. He had an IQ of 156, and since he was a preteen, he wanted to be an entrepreneur. He used to carry around a briefcase at age 12. His second job as a youth was working at a law firm.

My husband always put 110% into whatever he undertook, whether it was family, his career, working out, or the attainment of knowledge. We regularly cleaned the house, washed the cars and cooked as a family. Joseph consistently made an effort to better himself and motivate those around him to be more efficient. He often said, "It takes so much more energy to reverse one's momentum and return to motivate someone who is stagnating than to keep skyrocketing forward." Even so, he always backtracked to help someone else move forward in life. He would give people advice and listen patiently and curiously for hours with each friend, family member or business partner.

I considered him nearly perfect. I always told him, "If God allowed me to create my own man, I would not have created a being as perfect as you." He was strong, yet he knew how to self-examine, then if necessary, admit when he was wrong. He made a real effort not to commit the same offense twice. He was only wrong 5% of the time so when he was wrong, I would giggle and surmise, "He is human!"

He taught me how to face the challenging undertakings first. My nature was to avoid conflict at all cost; this was achieved by isolating, sleeping, and escaping through watching TV or staying busy with work, friends, or errands. I learned when I faced the hard tasks or situations first, I matured and flourished.

Joe would share about his amazing travels, his visions for our family, and his desire to change the consciousness of the world. I would actively listen while he shared his disappointments in the selfishness and greed of the people in the world. Joseph often contemplated what could cause a person to betray someone that only had their best interest at heart. Despite his frustration in human nature, he would always bounce back to his funny, serving, and kind-hearted demeanor. As he went through life's health challenges, we remained a team and grew stronger together. We were better together than apart. Even in his physical pain and suffering, he pushed on so much so, that outsiders would never know he was sick; he continued to smile and serve until the end.

CONTENTS

PREFACE

Joe taught me to search for the truth and confirm what I assimilated. He kindly instructed me to cease searching for happiness outside of myself. I took that advice and ran with it, and it was so empowering!

It's almost automatic for women to wait for their Prince Charming to come along and save them from all their problems. We have read enough books and seen enough movies to believe in this fairy tale. We need to realize that even if we had married Jesus Christ, Mohammad or Buddha, we would still have to do the work to fix and keep our lives on track.

If a person were sick due to malnutrition, she would have to take the vitamins, eat good foods and reduce the nutritionally deficient meals. It would not be her doctor's job to come to her house every day to make sure she takes her multi-vitamins or her spouse's job to fix her healthy lunches. In the same way, it is no one's job but your own, to uncover what makes you unhappy or discover your triggers and get the help to resolve them.

We can easily blame someone else for our unhappiness; this keeps us stuck. A person may trigger you, but the sadness was sitting there dormant – due to a connection to some abuse, neglect or a belief system that a person has about themselves that is destroying their future or causing them to limp through life. I tell you if you do the work, you won't have to just survive, You Can Thrive!

The Creator doesn't want us to get by in life. He wants us to thrive and experience the fullness of His blessings. Not only will He meet our needs, but His hope is for us to use our experiences to help pull others out of the pit of despair where we once were. To offer you hope it is the reason why I write this book exposing my hardships and pain, but also my triumphs, joy, and peace! Let's go on this adventure together!

When you start to open your mind, you will find peace, comfort, and that the answers to your dilemmas were all around you. The reason you never noticed it before, is you never really stopped to listen, or think deeply about what was said, or read about in an article or book or going on around you. You have to learn to slow down enough to see the miracles.

"All praises belong to the God and Father of our Lord Jesus Christ. For he is the Father of tender mercy and **the God of endless comfort. He always comes alongside us to comfort us in every suffering so that we can come alongside those who are in any painful trial. We can bring them this same comfort that God has poured out upon us.**"
2 Corinthians 1:3-4 The Passion Translation (TPT)

This is the way I see the above scripture come to life; here are just a few of the revelations. Have you ever been having a hard day and someone lets you go in front of them in a long line? On another day, you are feeling sad, and someone compliments you, and it makes you feel so warm inside. Or you had a bad day at work, and you come home, and your kid gives you a big hug or makes you laugh and the trouble of the day seems to fade away? That small gesture fills you up, and then you are able to be loving, joyful, and outwardly focused, and your strength has been renewed. Another scenario is you wonder why something happened and you hear a song or read a paragraph in an article that answers the question you were wrestling over. Another occurrence that people label as coincidence where God comforts you through someone else. When you are thinking of someone, and they call you a few minutes later, and they say something that you can relate to that makes you feel understood and not alone in the world. Have you ever gone to church and the sermon seems like somebody has been telling your business to the preacher? This is proof that God is listening and answering you.

INTRODUCTION

I have read many books about the effects of the hardness of hearts and the harm we inflict on one another trying to run from our pain. This book will give you healthy ways to deal with your pain instead of the ways the world tries to drown out what haunts them with drugs, alcohol, sex, or any other addiction.

I share in this book the thoughts and feelings not always expressed aloud or in constructive ways in marriage, and I provide some ideas of better ways to get the point across. This book discusses the challenges our youth face in school or once they walk out the door of their homes. I will have to point out hard events that happen in life because sometimes a person doesn't realize they were being abused emotionally, sexually, or physically. They figured it was discipline or love or what the norm is in families, especially if they were young when the event happened. The predator wants you to think what is happening is "normal" thus keeping the evil behavior going.

My goal in writing this book is to empower you, provide you tools and suggestions to begin your healing journey or resume your healing. Many of us start to try to heal and get an unhealthy therapist or get put on the wrong medications from a psychiatrist, and then we say, "This stuff does not work."

Most of us like food, right? Well, even though we all like a good meal, we all have our favorite foods, but not everyone's favorite food is the same. Your best friend adores chocolate ice cream, but you prefer cheesecake. They are both in the dessert category, but the way you respond to them is different how it makes you feel good, bad, or indifferent. Treatment for healing is like that.

If you were celebrating your birthday and someone brought you a bowl of brussels sprouts with a candle sticking out of the middle, you might not be too happy. You might say, "It is my birthday, and I want cake!" Then someone else brings you a cake, but it is sugar-free and gluten-free. You still might be unhappy even though they gave you what you asked for cake. This book will have various options to promote well-being, and you will have to figure out what works best for you since the book is applying across age groups, genders, and backgrounds.

Some methods work faster than others but may cost a little more. There are also healing therapies that work and are on a sliding pay scale and could only cost you $5 for the whole family, but the family must attend 14-16 sessions in total, attending one meeting every week. There are treatments that you would not even think deals with trauma but works fast. Another remedy that you can do on your own is with honesty in your journaling to get to the root of what you are feeling and what is fueling your actions. Another method of getting unstuck from negative comments repeated throughout your lifetime is by recording over the negative message playing in your mind, by repeating positive phrases, daily, out loud and silently to yourself to overcome self-esteem issues. No matter the time or the cost, once healed, it will be worth every cent and every minute of your precious time. The way you think has to be changed, and you cannot do it alone if it is caused by trauma. I don't want to get into too much detail right now; I want you to be surprised at all the new ways to better your life.

I know some of you worry about unlocking all the things you have kept buried for so long. I found that the circumstances I was afraid of were more terrifying in my head than in real life. Sometimes the things I worried about or feared occurred; they were challenging but not obliterating, as long as I looked at it from the right perspective. I have shared my stories with many people in the last 21 years of my life. It gave them strength and made them feel more grateful for what they went through. It could have been worse for any of us even though it was hard and unfair, but like me, they will make it through and come out better people if they choose to learn instead of growing bitter.

Life's most significant challenges help people learn about themselves and how strong they can be or discover their weaknesses. The feat is learning to accept the admirable along with the shameful. The next step in the development process is learning to give grace to others when you see their mistakes and deficiencies. Learning to see the good in yourself and others, realizing cooperation is better than conflict.

Most regrets come from mindless reactions rather than poor planning. Of course, I am not saying do not stand up for what is right or don't protect yourself or speak up when people are out of line. I want you to stand up for yourself and others. I am just saying some people fight first, last and always. You have to pick your battles. Not everything is worth a fight. In the cases when it is not worth the struggle, and you find yourself getting upset (habitually reactive), you need to learn to think objectively. Sometimes, if you cannot physically remove yourself from the situation, you will have to use your mind to transport yourself to a calm, peaceful environment to reset your emotions. This is when stopping what you are doing and take a slow and full deep breath filling your lungs from the top to the bottom will be of great benefit - breathing in from your nose and out of your mouth visualizing negative energy releasing as you blow out and a blue light of calm when you breathe in.

CHAPTER ONE

CHOICES

Everything in life is a choice of how a person will respond to life knocking them around or lifting them up. You may feel an ache or emptiness or something is wrong, but you cannot quite put your finger on it. To heal, you have to do a self-examination.

When you have pain, or you don't feel well, you go to a doctor to get an examination. Some of you go onto the Internet and do a symptom search and self-diagnosis. I do not recommend Internet self-diagnosis because you do not have the educational background or the expertise to analyze all the information. You will end up treating yourself but not getting better; after the situation has worsened, then you will finally go to the doctor.

Since you don't know what is wrong with you, it can be difficult to know what type of doctor to visit. Do you need an Orthopedic doctor, Neurologist, Pulmonologist, or Cardiologist, or Rheumatologist? Before you go into the doctor, you will need a list of your symptoms.

The list of questions below will sort through what you honestly feel. It is important to notice where do you feel the emotions when they come up - in your back, neck, chest, stomach, throat or head, etc.? You might want to write your answers down in a journal to keep track of what you discover. Your first response will probably be the closest to the truth, or you may need more time to think of some of these questions and answers will come to you later.

Louise Hay, author of "You Can Heal Your Life," does a great job of identifying the message the body is giving through specific symptoms. If you have aches – this could mean you need to be held or you feel a lack of love. If you feel pain in your back – your body could be telling you that you don't feel supported in life or a particular situation. If the pain is in the lower part of your back, this usually represents a lack of financial support. If the tightness or pain is in the middle of your back, it represents guilt. If the symptoms are in the upper back, you lack emotional support, or you feel unloved. If you get headaches when certain subjects come up, this represents self-criticism, and fear. If you have a tight neck or pain, this represents inflexibility and stubbornness or refusing to see the other side of a situation.

Pain always seeks punishment, so pain represents guilt. Stomach problems represent dread and fear of change. Tightness in the throat or a sore throat represents swallowed rage, refusal to move forward, stagnate creativity, and the inability to speak up for oneself.

This world is not very good at putting words to feelings or even dealing with feelings head-on. We tend to avoid, push down and medicate our feelings because that is what we witnessed how others dealt with their pain. We also judge the comments and reactions to our agony which caused us to conclude that emotions are not relevant or they are a sign of weakness.

Are you happy?
Do you want to be happy?
Do you think you deserve to be happy?
Are you convinced that what you think or feel matters or is important?

3

Do you love others unconditionally? Do you feel like that is how they love you?

Can you quickly come up with a list of why you like or love yourself?

Do you feel accepted?

Do you feel like you are always chasing acceptance, approval or to be considered worthy?

Do you love yourself the way you want others to respond to you?

Do you have close friends, family or both who REALLY know who you are - the good, the bad, and the ugly? Do they love you anyway?

Are you looking for someone, or some accomplishment to fill the void you have inside?

Do you trust your decisions?

Do you respect yourself?

Do you expect others to treat you with respect or are you a doormat?

Do you put yourself down or beat yourself up verbally or in your mind?

Can you accept a compliment?

Do you feel tired all the time?

Are you angry most of the time?

Do you feel more than one or two emotions?

What is the emotion you feel most of the time?

Do you like your body?

Can you look in the mirror and be pleased with what you see?

Are you overweight a lot or a little?

Do you think you are overweight but you are not?

Do you starve yourself?

Do you vomit on purpose?

Do you not eat when you are depressed?

Do you eat junk foods when you are angry?

Do you drink alcohol when things aren't going your way?

Do most of your friends consume alcohol? So, you do the same?

Are you an isolated drinker?

Do you look in the mirror only to point out everything that is wrong with yourself?

Do you trust people?

Do you feel safe?

Do you know what a "Safe Person" is?

Do you have healthy boundaries?

Do you even know what boundaries are?

Have you ever given your whole heart to someone? Could you do it again easily?

Are your dating relationships healthy in the past or the present?

Do you avoid dating altogether?

Does your partner respect you?

Do you think all one gender is defective?

Do you feel comfortable to say, "No" to anything?

Are your relationships short or long lasting and fulfilling?

Do you only feel worthy when you are in a relationship, no matter if the alliance is healthy for you or not?

Do you give in to other people's wishes more than you would like to? Are you worried that people won't like you?

Do you feel loved for who you are, or are you hiding part of who you are because you foresee you won't be looked at the same way if you exposed it?

Does everyone you date have the same personality type - controlling, insecure, jealous, violent or lacking in verbal self-control?

Do you have parent/child relationships with your dating partner?

Do you have a negative experience from childhood that still affects you today? (Unprocessed memory.)

A human being does not have self-esteem problems coming out of the womb. We enter this world loving who we are, from our heads to our toes. Not bonding with our mother at birth due to a health issue involving the mother or the child, not being touched or held enough because you are in an incubator for a month or longer at the beginning of one's life can cause issues that you cannot pinpoint. Being delivered by C-section can cause trauma coming into the world that will affect the baby. The mother is lethargic due to medication or pain which interferes with the beginning bonding stage between mother and child. The mother, having postpartum depression, can leave a baby feeling like he or she is not good enough or unloved.

Being raised by an alcoholic or drug-addicted parent can fill a child with fear or loneliness or cause the homelife to be unstable which would steal a child's confidence and safety. It could be that they never listened to you or talked to you about your day or your feelings. These feelings affect how you interact with others which will have a tremendous effect on your dating life. You will tend to gravitate to a partner that lacks self-control, has anger issues, or is emotionally withdrawn, a poor listener and repeats your upbringing. I have found that far too many of us look for happiness outside ourselves, in a relationship or a car, a house, a job title, a promotion, a particular salary or specific body dimensions. We won't always be young or healthy, but you can choose to be happy. Some people think that if they get a successful, good-looking partner, it will help them feel worthy or better about themselves. You might have a marvelous partner, but if you are insecure, you will always be working hard to keep that person or be fearful you will lose that person. If you do lose that person, then you will feel even worse about yourself because you never thought you were good enough for them or deserved them or you were pretending to be whatever they wanted you to be and weren't valuing who you are.

Being happy starts with you; loving yourself, respecting yourself, learning to solve your problems, maturing, and learning to take constructive criticism. You also should learn to toss away the statements from people who are jealous or envious of you and that want to tear you down. If you don't know yourself, you won't know when someone is lying or telling you the truth because you won't trust your gut feelings.

You may feel tired all the time because you have a lot of fear, anxiety, worries due to having a parent who was critical, or had emotional health issues or yelled a lot or maybe there was a lot of drama in your household. The anxiety could cause you to have eating abnormalities. You could have an upset stomach from continual stress which causes you not to eat, so you are underweight.

Some people are anorexic or bulimic because someone when they were growing up, said they would be fat because it is in their genes. A child could have been told that they were overweight when they were not; this caused the child to see themselves incorrectly or be fearful of food or gaining weight.

Sexual abuse or unresolved childhood trauma is known to be the cause for bulimia, but it is on an unconscious level. Louise Hay defines "anorexia as the body message that there is extreme fear, self-hatred, and self-rejection. Bulimia is the body saying there is hopelessness, terror, and self-hatred."

People with anorexia nervosa restrict their food intake and end up dying of starvation. The disturbing part about it is no matter how thin they get they still see themselves as fat. After a while, the message of hunger turns off. "Nine out of ten people with anorexia are females. 1% of American females from age 10 to 25 are anorexic. They tend to be overachievers and perfectionist," said WebMD.

If you started modeling at a young age, the industry's goal is the clothes should hang on the person like their body is a hanger. This mentality is one reason there is an obsession over weight and food. They also can be obsessive about exercise in an unhealthy way. Actors may look normal on TV, but in real life, they can be under-weight. It is said that the camera adds ten pounds to a person. Then our young people look at these fashion shows on TV and in the magazines and

8

think that is what is normal and they start to become insecure about their bodies when they are a right size for their height and age BMI (Body Mass Index). The models weigh themselves daily or every other day and stress about gaining a pound. The fields of acting, modeling, dancing, and sports overemphasize the body image. A sickly, mal-nutrition child is not going to be successful for long. They will end up being admitted to the hospital or worse. We as a society have to start caring more about our people than our profits.

You may use food to fill the void of loneliness, not being understood or past traumas, so now you wear your weight as a barrier from people. You may not even know why you feel hungry all the time, or you know you are full, but you keep eating anyway; this is emotional eating. Some people eat a lot because that is the only way they got attention from their family when they were young, and as an adult, it is an unconscious habit.

The other reason you could be hungry often is because your body is getting food but not nutrition and you will need to boost your intake of vitamin/ mineral enriched foods into your daily routine. Did you know that the human body needs 90 different vitamins and minerals a day to be healthy? Dr. Joel Wallach, the founder of Youngevity, has a lot of great lectures regarding vitamins, minerals, and health.

The American diet today on average is not getting these essential nutrients daily. Even if we do take vitamins in tablets, most of the minerals aren't absorbed in our bodies. We need to take liquid vitamins and minerals, or gel caps or powder versions so a majority of these illness preventing nutrients will be utilized. Even if we eat a lot of fruits and vegetable, the fact that our soil is depleted of nutrients due to overgrowing foods in the soil continually means there are no vitamins and minerals left in the ground to be absorbed into the fruits and vegetables to meet our bodies daily requirements. Diseases are caused by deficiencies, toxins, and stress. The number one way to change your life is by eating better foods, getting exercise to reduce stress and flush out toxins and detoxing and learning to deal with situations more constructively.

We cannot change the past, but we can change how we react to it, and our attitudes about it. You can either be one of these scenarios below or something better. We tend to make a lot of decisions out of habit. Acknowledging the issues takes it from the subconscious and puts it in the conscience so you can make better choices.

"Of them the proverbs are true: "A dog **returns to its vomit**," and, "A sow that is washed returns to her **wallowing in the mud**." 2 Peter 2:22 New International Version (NIV)

Do you consider three months or a year is a long relationship? Do you feel like you don't know your companion any better a year later than you knew that person when you first started dating? This is a red flag. Either they are hiding something, or they are shallow but either way, with more time, it is not going to get any better.

Do you want to keep being involved with boyfriends that use your body like they own you and you have no say about what is happening to you? Do you want to keep dating guys that used to pay for gifts, dinners, and dates for you when you first started dating, but now your admirer hardly ever takes you out and is always borrowing money from you for what he or she wants? This is a character defect you want to avoid and to work through whatever is in you that attracted this kind of person to you.

Perhaps, you want to be loved so much; you will date someone you are not attracted to just because they show you attention. Are you not ok with the thought of being alone? If you feel you need to be with someone to be worthy or feel special, your self-esteem, self-worth, self-respect needs some attention. The area where you don't think highly of yourself needs your focus before you give that focus to the opposite sex or for some, the same gender.

Do you find yourself wearing your hair the way your suitor likes instead of what makes you feel beautiful? Do you not wear the dress to a party you picked out because he said you should wear the other one? It is alright if you need help with your fashion sense, but if this is a constant thing, the red flags have turned to sirens.

Do you want to return to an abusive relationship that repeats how your abusive parent treated you? Do you want to continue being disrespected or cussed at by your boyfriend or husband only to get the courage to leave them finally, but because you did not do the work to heal, yourself you find a new boyfriend/

girlfriend or spouse with most of the bad qualities you just walked away from? Do you want to continue the cycle of cheating boyfriends because your father always cheated on your mom, and you believe that is all that exists in the world? You could be a new parent and all the poor parenting you received as a child comes rushing in, making you doubt your ability to be a good parent. Do you want to keep feeling guilty, dirty, not good enough and having no peace? Or are you ready for a CHANGE?

You may think, "Well my life was pretty drama free in my family." The issue could be a comment from a teacher from elementary school who implied you are not so bright or not as pretty as the other girls because you were overweight. Being young, you accepted what authority figures said as accurate.

Maybe, your companion left you, and you are having a hard time processing those feelings. It could be that you have never been married and are getting older and it causes you to question yourself. Do you find yourself saying what you think your sweetheart wants to hear instead of expressing your own opinion hoping that this will help you hold onto him? Are you hiding how brilliant you are because you have found men to be threatened by your intellect? Are you willing to give up your career to be a housewife just so your fiancé won't call off the engagement? I know that in church you might have heard women are the helpers of men, but that doesn't mean that we have to give up who we are to be with them. You might have heard we are the weaker sex, that might be true physically but not in every area. Women have a destiny and purpose for why they are here, and it is not to be a door mat for a man. I am all for partners for life and dating, but the relationship should grow each person involved in the relationship, not be one-sided.

You had a layoff at a job, and it damaged your confidence or self-worth. Maybe, you did not get laid off, but many of your friends did, and it had an impact leaving a residue of fear and insecurity. Or you have been in a job most of your life but have been passed over for promotions many times. This takes digging to see what the company values or your department or boss thinks is most important; then you have to ask yourself are you doing those things consistently. Could it be that you are in management, but you are not fulfilled? Another worthwhile question is what made you get into that field? Perhaps it was just something everyone in your family did; be a lawyer, doctor or work in the family business. What is it that would fulfill you? Maybe your job is excellent, the people are friendly, and the pay is terrific, but it takes too much of your time, so you don't have a social life. Maybe, you can stop volunteering for so many projects or delegate some of the work to others to free up your time. Only you know what is acceptable in your field, but it could be your job lacks proper boundaries and needs to hire more people. It might be time to find work and life balance. Whatever the reason, isn't it about time you started healing from it or making decisions to bring more joy into your life?

"There is a time for everything, and a season for every activity under the heavens:

A time to be born and a time to die,
A time to plant and a time to uproot,
A time to kill and **a time to heal,**
A time to tear down and **a time to build**,
A time to weep and **a time to laugh**,
A time to mourn and **a time to dance**,
A time to scatter stones and a time to gather them,
A time to embrace and a time to refrain from embracing,
A time to search and a time to give up,
A time to keep and **a time to throw away**,
A time to tear and **a time to mend**,
A time to be silent and **a time to speak**,
A time to love and a time to hate,
A time for war and **a time for peace**." Ecclesiastes 3:1-8 New International Version (NIV)

When is it your time for these things in bold? Haven't you spent enough time in sorrow, suffering, regrets, pain, humiliation, isolation, loneliness, fear, anger, self-pity, blame and holding onto what is not good for you? Isn't it time to throw those old thought patterns away that don't serve you? It does not matter what someone said or did or what you said or did; you don't have to live in your or their past shortcomings. You can have an existence far from the world you knew. You can look different, feel better and be what you want to be. Old patterns can change if you take action to revamp your thoughts which, will in turn, improve your efforts.

Don't you want to search your heart for what makes you happy? Don't you want to love others with your whole heart and have that healthy, unconditional love returned to you? Don't you want to heal? When was the last time you laughed? When was the last time you said what you felt or what you wished you would have said? Was it never?

Webster's dictionary says "caring means feeling or showing concern for or showing kindness to others." We can care for others. We lay down our lives for our children, and no matter what they do we always forgive them. We put up with whatever drama comes from our spouse or lovers or friends in high school or college, and we let it go. At the same time, we struggle with feeling compassion for ourselves, forgiving ourselves or even taking care of oneself. Believe it or not, when we don't care for ourselves enough, we don't care for others in the best way we are capable like setting limits, healthy boundaries and teaching them to respect us. You may find that you have ok boundaries when it comes to other people but cannot tell yourself, "No."

Poor boundaries are at the root of all these symptoms: depression, anxiety, eating disorders, addictions, impulsive disorders, guilt problems, shame issues, panic disorders, and marital and relationship struggles. Boundaries are anything that helps you define you from someone else.

"Wounds from a friend can be trusted, but an enemy multiplies kisses." Proverbs 27:6 New International Version (NIV)

I like this scripture because I think if a friend will tell you, you are heading in the wrong direction health-wise when you are ten pounds overweight, you will never get to be forty pounds overweight. It takes some time to go from being a bombshell physique to weighing 200 lbs. You have to love someone enough to want the best for them even if it will hurt their feelings and they get mad at you or stop talking to you. We have to start conditioning our minds to acknowledge people telling us the truth; that truth is constructive love. I am not saying to accept every comment as valid from a 7friend who is a pessimist. I am not even saying if no one confirms you can achieve your goal that you should stop pursuing your dreams. In the beginning, when you are changing old patterns, you may only find one person who believes in you more than you do. It is a good start. You are further along than when you started.

You must ask yourself, "Are my friends healthy for me or helping me stay stuck?" When you are starting to make progress does your friend sabotage you? Is your friend hurtful with the truth that facilitates your advancement or does their words restrain you? Do not think that they are your friends if they lie to you to avoid hurting your feelings.

Remember who was there for you. Who tried to help you and pushed you to be better? I want you to nurture these relationships. These are your friends and the safe people. A healthy support system is critical during this point in your healing from low self-esteem, self-image issues, and trust issues, etc.

When you feel good about yourself, other people who feel good about themselves will gravitate to you. You will find your life funnier, happier, and more peaceful. People will serve you and want to help you, and they will give you words of encouragement. You will start getting things you always wanted. It will be like making a wish when you blow out the candle on a cake, but the results will show up.

I love flowers, and when I started working on myself, I got all kinds of flowers from different men and women to encourage me, not to try to date me, ok maybe some of the men wanted to date me. When I was in healthy relationships in my past, they gave me flowers and gifts and did marvelous, memorable things with me. If you don't love yourself, you will push these kinds of people away because you think you don't deserve it. You will sabotage your healthy relationships.

What I ask of you is to start to care for yourself by you taking an active part in healing from your past. Caring is doing what is best for ourselves and others. If you saw your child sabotaging himself/herself or not living up to their full potential because you care about them, wouldn't you say something? Wouldn't you try to point them in the right direction? If you would do it for others, why wouldn't you do it for yourself? Haven't you let this pain from your past limit your life long enough?

If you believe this is a waste of time and do not give it your best, it will be a waste of time for you. When a person's faith is active, their trust makes things happen. The power of the mind is mighty. You have to train it to work for you, not against you. It is like trying to go on a diet for your mother or because your husband asked you to, but for you, your weight is not an issue. Every time you are out of their sight you sneak a donut or two or binge on ice cream or whatever your choice of self-indulgence is. If you do not have healthy outlets for yourself, when you are sad, disappointed or feeling a lot, you will backslide. This reverse in progress does not only apply to diets.

If you don't already know how you are going to deal with the hurt, anger, shame, guilt, or self-criticism, you will turn to something worse. I have had moments when I was too discouraged or too faithless to pray. In those moments, I would crave a cigarette, which I have not had since 10th grade, but if I had kept that habit up, it would have one day turned to health challenges, cancer and eventually death.

The emotional or mental abuse that you do to yourself or someone else has done to you has caused enough pain. We have to take our power back and make better choices. Now when I am upset, I guzzle a big bottle of Smart Water. It is pH balanced water that is good for me that holds the vitamins and minerals in but releases the toxins out my temple. If I guzzle a big bottle of juice or soda, in the end, I will gain weight or develop diabetes. Life is full of causes and effects. We have to get out of the momentary pleasure seeking and look long term.

Let's look at some scenarios where we judge ourselves or others. We need to accept ourselves without passing judgment on ourselves or other people. You might get good grades in all your subjects except in one class that is difficult for you. How easy or hard something is a matter of perspective. If you are a Super Jock – P.E. is a snap, but for someone who sits a lot due to studying or playing an instrument for hours or has health issues, physical activities could be very challenging. For those of you who like to learn or have a gift in the areas of math and science such as biology, chemistry, and statistics or physics, they could be effortless. For those who are tone deaf, the choir is a struggle. Everyone has their talents and gifts. That is why we need each other to bring balance to the world.

Where would we be on Sunday without football, baseball, basketball, and soccer games? For some of these athletes, math or English are challenging classes, and they barely graduate, but as you know, they can become a huge success. For others, being social is a challenge, but they create astonishing things in the world. Then we have that shy person that comes alive when he or she plays music or dances or sings. They are needed to bring us joy, to make us dance or sooth our souls.

Some of the heavier people are the greatest cooks. When we eat their food, our mouth sings, and our spirit soars! There are other people, the only class they were good at was woodshop, and they left school before graduating. These same people make our furniture, our statues, and breathtaking art.

We can make false judgments about ourselves and the world. We may be the prettiest in our high school but average in a group of top models. What does it matter? No one is perfect even though many of us are taught to strive for perfection. This mindset keeps us dissatisfied, disappointed and not living in the moment or appreciating the achievements in life. We can have a habit of just moving onto the next thing on our list instead of taking the time to enjoy the goal achieved. How unfulfilling and sad!

Some of the people who have the most going for them are the ones who feel the need to belittle others to make themselves feel better about who they are. How unfortunate! Some of the wealthiest people are the unhappiest people, always competing and worrying who will take their spot as the best whatever. They don't know how to relax even on their vacations; their minds cannot be silenced. Meditation and Mindfulness are great practices to manage this.

Webster's dictionary says, "Confidence is a feeling or consciousness of one's powers and the quality or state of being certain and the relation of trust or intimacy." Most of us are not blind, deaf, paralyzed, physically impaired yet we complain every day about the little things not realizing how lucky we are. These bad habits can lead to anxiety, depression and being overly focused on the negative. Exercise is good for relieving stress and building confidence in one's self. Yoga is good for releasing pushed down feelings and for Type A personalities and replaces the tension with relaxation, a calmer mind, and gets those unhealthy dormant emotions and experiences out of the tissues.

Please drink plenty of water before and after any exercises. Otherwise, dehydration makes your brain look like a brain on drugs. Those of you who take water pills to slim down, please stop, because it is not good for your mind. I am not talking about what a doctor sees on an MRI or CAT Scan but what shows up on a 3D Brain SPECT. A SPECT scan evaluates 55 areas of your brain, looking for over or under activity or a vibrant membrane. Healthy tissue is smooth but a dehydrated brain has indentions, or it looks like holes in your brain. Our mind runs our whole body; please treat it with love, respect, and protection.

The people with physical challenges inspires us to look at the bright side, not to give up when we face uncertainty, to count our blessings and get out of our ungrateful, victim mentality. They can put us to shame with how hard they fight to do the little things and how happy they are most of the time. I know many special needs children and no matter how hard it is for them to communicate or move certain body parts they smile, laugh, and keep trying. I have noticed that special needs kids smile more often than typical teenagers who are more fortunate. I have discovered one of the major causes for this is the typical kids' minds are trapped in a place of entitlement. In chapter seven, I will give you affirmations to reverse this mentality. We have to see the value in everyone. Arrogance, bullying, and prejudice is just a way to hide fears, weaknesses, and lack of knowledge about a particular area.

Confidence is also believing in yourself without having to put others down. There should be no comparing yourself to anyone else except to use that information to help you make decisions. These are the great things that can happen if you choose a different path. A great example of overcoming predicaments is Michael J. Fox. He was succeeding in life, and then he got Parkinson's disease. He did not let it stop him from acting when he started discovering symptoms during his performances in "Spin City." Mr. Fox did not deny what he went through; Michael felt it, and then he revealed his health situation to the world. Dealing with full-blown Parkinson's, he came back to do a wonderful role in "Designated Survivor." In life, Mr. Fox became an activist for funding and pushing for more research to be done, regarding tackling Parkinson's. He raised about $750 million thus having a positive influence on society and especially, those battling with this ailment.

Again, comparing yourself to others is ok when you use it to make better choices - for example, thinking that this is what will happen to my life if I take this wrong path or don't do anything to resolve this debilitating situation. We are bombarded with bad news every day with the tragedies of the people we admire taking the road of drugs, alcohol or suicide. No further explanation needs to be expressed about the consequences of not dealing with life's struggles in a productive manner.

For people who are shy and have a hard time in social situations; if you don't believe me that you matter, then you should get out more, interact more often, or take a communications class, so you don't feel so awkward in conversations; you will see for yourself you matter. Learn to understand body language so you can see when discussions are making people feel uncomfortable. It also helps you understand your emotions. Everyone has weakness and insecurities with practice makes for improvement and comfortability. I use to be so shy but no one would call me shy now. I made an effort to change when I saw it was not benefiting me. I am not saying I never have fear, but I face it and do the action anyway because it is what I want and I don't want fear holding me back from enjoying life and trying new things.

We have to learn to be content where we are, but willing to move forward to be better. If you don't get everything done in one day be happy about what you did get done instead of beating yourself up over the two tasks you missed doing on a list of 12 things. For those of you whose list is smaller, there might only be 4 or 5 things, but they are big things that take much time and effort. Learn to relax and enjoy your life! Delight in who you are!

CHAPTER TWO

EXPOSING THE TRUTH

You may ask yourself, "Why am I still thinking about this?" The event or events happened decades ago. What is wrong with me? Doesn't time heal all wounds?

We shall begin again with digging. Please answer these questions as truthfully as you can. Please write your answers in a journal.

Are you afraid of the dark?

Are you afraid to be home alone?

Do you avoid parties?

Do you jump when someone touches you?

Do you cuddle after intimacy or do you turn away because of shame or other negative feelings?

Do you wish you could be someone else -anyone else?

Is everyone substandard to you; even if you won't admit it out loud, do you think it?

Do you make excuses not to be intimate with your partner?

Do you have sex because you want to or your partner wants to?

Do you make love or is it just sex?

Do you feel free to say "NO" to sex?

Is the only way for you to feel "loved" is by having sex?

Have you ever had an orgasm?

Do you have to fantasize to have an orgasm?

Is the only thing that makes you orgasm, is having power over someone else?

Do you secretly wonder if you are gay because you don't enjoy sex?

Do you fantasize about S & M because you want to punish someone or to feel powerful? Do you feel you need to be punished? Do you think you are broken? Do you have nightmares? Have you been having the same nightmare for years? Do you have sexual triggers that cause fear, nausea, shame, disgust, or anything unpleasant?

Do you have nightmares after seeing a movie or TV program where someone is raped or molested?

Do you want to run away or stuff your feelings or do you get angry and out of control after reading a story, listening to the news, or seeing a TV show or movie where someone is raped or molested, kidnapped or physically abused?

Do you avoid relationships with people who have similarities to your abuser (height, body build, skin color, hair color, or ethnicity)?

Does the sound of someone's voice make you cringe because it has an eerie commonality to your abuser?

Do you avoid places that remind you of your abuse (a type of car, color of a car, a park, a neighborhood or music by an exact artist because it was playing when you were attacked)?

Have you stopped wearing skirts, or dresses or stretch pants because that is what you were wearing when you were brutalized?

Do you feel you matter - that you add value to this world?

27

If you are afraid of the dark because you were mugged in the evening or you were molested in the middle of the night when everyone else was asleep. You are justified in your fear what you feel matters! Did someone break into your family's home and assault you while they were out at a movie or on a date? Your fear of being home alone is a natural response to whatever was the actual scenario. Did you use to enjoy parties until one evening you drank too much, and you found yourself left in a room half naked not remembering what happened or the guy's name you were talking with that night. Worried you might run into him again or someone just like him at another party, your mind is trying to protect you with that fear. The only problem is that fear is overlapping into other areas of your life and stealing your feelings of safety.

Do you have nightmares that are just images or flashes but it feels genuine? Those are probably memories of a terrible event that your body has buried to protect you. In order for the nightmares to go away, you have to see a professional about it and try to retrieve the rest of the story so the memory can be processed. EMDR (Eye Movement Desensitization Reprocessing) is good at recovering memories and taking the fear or negative emotions away.

You may never see the person that hurt you again, but reminders of them will show up in other people. Someone you don't know may wear the same cologne, someone in a crowd may have the same laugh, you may see your predator in someone else their hair color or height or body build. The girl you like may touch you the way that babysitter did that molested you, and then you find yourself no longer returning your girlfriend's calls. Trust me this is one of the most challenging things about this kind of crime.

Sex was invented to help you bond with that other person and be soulmates for life but in this case that meshing was with a villain. The only thing I can advise on this subject is whoever has a similar feature or preference they are not the person who hurt you. There are almost 7 billion people on this Earth; there are going to be commonalities between us, humans. How many times can a sperm/egg combination split and get something 100% completely different? There are only so many products; someone is going to like the same brand as your predator or like the same music etc.

There is nothing wrong with you. You are normal. There is something sick and twisted about the predator; this is a clinical description, perverted, domineering, hostile, sadistic and insane. "Once a predator is drunk or on drugs, they are no longer able to restrain their impulses; a trigger could be feeling disrespected or threatened in any way." People like this are released from prison because the laws have not been updated. This is where the change has to occur. These offenders always repeat their crimes no matter how long it takes months or years to the detriment of law-abiding citizens. The citizens of America get no warning of these released repeat offenders and no police or authority figures check up on them like the citizens get notified where a child molester is living when they are released from prison. These criminals are released even at the doctor's advice against it. "The reporting team is reviewing the records of more than

600 people that the Psychiatric Security Review Board has placed in community programs or set free over the last 10 years," based on a ProPublica article by Jayme Fraser, The Malheur Enterprise on April 25, 2018, called A Sick System: Oregon Doctors Warned That a Killer and Rapist Would Likely Attack Again. Then the State Released Him.

Those who endure abuse tend not to know how they are feeling. Your body usually will tell you. Learn to look in the mirror. When you think you are smiling, look in the mirror you might be surprised that it is not a smile. We have become desolate or robot-like for so long, we forget how to smile or show genuine happiness. Even when we feel happy, we might hide it. We could be afraid someone will steal our joy if they know what makes us happy.

The reason why I ask all these questions is that I have found that a small percentage of people do not remember being abused or they do not think it was abuse. A significant boundary is where you begin, which is your skin that is your property line. Being abused taught us that our property did not start at our skin because someone did whatever they wanted to our bodies. We have to learn how to build a good, sturdy fence with words. Notice I did not say a wall. With a fence, you can let the good in and kick the bad out. You are in control of your property!

When someone is saying something, you don't like; you can walk in your house and leave them at the gate. It gives you that needed time and emotional distance to mend from the unhealthy behavior of others. Your action of withdrawing teaches that person their behavior is unacceptable. You don't have to deal with them when they are like that. It builds a strong foundation announcing that what you feel matters. It enforces that you make your own choices. You learn to set limits on those negative recordings that are like acid that eats away at you. It demonstrates you are in control of the thoughts you allow to affect you. This action screams, "I love and value myself, and if you are not going to be respectful, I will not have anything to do with you."

There is something that sticks out regarding potential victims to the predators. Usually, if you have been a victim once, you will be again. That is why we have to get healed so that we do not stand out like a "sign across our chests." I will use the word "we" a lot because I don't want you to feel like you are going through this alone. A person isolates when he or she thinks it is only me. We don't reach out or get help because we believe no one will understand.

The criminals look for the weak, the distracted, the easy prey, the shy, the people who get picked on but will not stand up for themselves or report it. We have to learn to be ok with that boundary of "NO." They scope out the loners, or someone drunk or high that might not remember their faces or enough details for the predator to get caught. I want to emphasize that drinking or being shy or a peacemaker does not make it your fault. Lions hunt and cobras strike; you just might have been in the wrong place at the wrong time. You might have even taken self-defense classes, but you were too scared or caught off guard to use what

31

you learned. You made it out of the situation alive, and that is a magnificent and victorious thing!

You can heal, and you can have a better life than you once had. Do not set a time limit. Do not say, it is taking years, or I thought I was over it and then this memory popped up, or I reacted poorly to a particular situation. It is like grief, the anniversaries of the memories will bring up feelings, but eventually, it won't feel like it just happened today or yesterday instead of years ago. Please be patient with yourself.

The way that I was rescued from abuse was not by my parents, or the neighbor reporting it, or me confiding in the principal of the school. It was through the scriptures. If I had not picked up the Bible and began to read it from cover to cover at age 12, I would have never known that what was happening to me during the summer was a crime. Even though that particular scripture was not talking about the same gender, the scripture still delivered the message I needed to know. Without this insight and strength through God to confront my abuser, my life could have turned out very differently. I am not saying the one-time use of the scriptures solved my problems in an instant. It took the reading of Leviticus to see the truth and the foundation of a good support system, which I did not have in my home. I also held onto the belief in the promises of God, and they made me bold.

"Do not have intercourse with an aunt, whether she is your father's sister or your mother's sister." Leviticus 18:12-13 New International Version (NIV)

Honesty starts by telling yourself the truth. It was amazing that the Bible taught me about incest, molestation and rape. I guess these things are as old as war and just as damaging.

"...An **honest person is** as **brave** as a lion". Proverbs 28:1.5 Good News Translation (GNT)

When I confronted my abuser, I was exposing him to the errors of his ways so that he had the opportunity to change. It was not my responsibility to make him have a transformation. It was just up to me to make sure that he would not continue to abuse me. I advise people not to go alone to confront a perpetrator. I opposed him during the abuse and stopped the act right then and there. Later in a letter, from a safe distance of 2,000 miles away, I presented the facts to him in more detail. Keep in mind if I could do it over, I would have exposed him in person with the authorities.

"We stayed in Athens and sent Timothy to get you up and about, cheering you on so **you wouldn't be discouraged by these hard times.**" 1 Thessalonians 3:3 The Message (MSG)

I want people to comprehend; when a person gets discouraged, it can be hard to get out of bed or function like they usually do. When a person has to have an awkward conversation, they need that trusted, reliable, fearless authority figure to go with them to give them strength to do what is necessary. Some people may not like police officers or authority figures because these authority figures have hurt them in the past. The choice of who supports you is up to you, as long as that person has proper boundaries and will protect you. They need to keep you from making unwise emotional decisions. When a person uncovers their past, they can have erratic emotions or be fully functional but devoid of emotions. Each person has learned to deal with pain differently.

In the past, I was too afraid to report the crimes committed against me because the mentality was different regarding abuse and the law treated "the innocent person" like "the temptress" and the "predator" like "the helpless victim to his bodily urges." The violated person feels like "she is at fault" instead of the other way around. This is not justice; it is NOT right, and it will Never be the truth.

"You will know the truth, and the **truth will set you free**." John 8:32 Christian Standard Bible (CSB)

I read an article that proves around the world things are not so different from when I was a teenager. Here is the story. "In January 2018, Artyom Iskhakov, a 19-year-old Russian man, killed his roommate and former girlfriend, Tatyana Strakhova, who was also 19. Following the murder, he raped her body and then, before killing himself, confessed in a letter published on Russia's most popular social networking site, VKontakte. According to Iskhakov's note, he was motivated by jealousy. As the story spread, commentators across Russia took to blaming Strakhova for her own murder. Some published photographs of the young woman with alcohol and cigarettes, or in her underwear, which they presented as evidence that she was at least partially guilty for inciting the attack. In an article detailing her Instagram activity, meanwhile, the Russian online publication *Dni.ru* noted that "Tanya Strakhova turned out to be less innocent than everyone thought." Some commenters on Strakhova's Instagram page even suggested that Iskhakov was, in fact, the victim—provoked by Strakhova into killing her."

Things need to change on a global scale. Even if Tanya Strakhova was a prostitute that gives no one the right to rape or kill her, but she wasn't, and you read how society turned on her instead of the predator? Things haven't changed much in this area since I was a teenager regarding the unfairness of how the world handles justice for the victim. It doesn't give justice. I feel sorry for the parents who had to read these terrible lies about their daughter. It shows how sick and twisted our minds have become in the world.

Have you ever had a bad feeling when you met someone, and that sensation warned you that they were going to hurt you, but it did not tell you when or how? I had a vision right before I started college, of being date raped by someone I worked with, and I pushed it away thinking that was too horrible to be real. That very day the incident happened. If I had listened to the warning, I could have avoided being raped. We get these "Red Flags" and only in hindsight do we say, "we should have listened." We have to learn to trust these messages since God knows everything; He loves us enough to provide a way out and to avoid the pain altogether. But because we don't trust our feelings or ourselves, we ignore them.

I was warned by a feeling that my boyfriend was not telling the truth, but I did not know what the lie was. I told my friends about this feeling. They told me that I was distrusting because of my past. Later, after I married this man, I found that the feelings were right and he lied about so many things. It damaged my trust in everyone, and it set me back financially, materially, spiritually, emotionally and physically. It took me about seven years to get over the pain of not listening to my gut feelings. I see now that I might have had a guardian angel watching over me, but I must learn to listen to the warnings. After much heartache of not listening to that voice of caution, I have finally learned to listen to that soft voice in my head more often.

The truth will set you free and save your life. Remember the worst-case scenario of abuse is you become the abuser to someone else, maybe not sexually, but emotionally or physically. The other equally monstrous situation we want to avoid, is you committing suicide. None of these options are places you want to go.

My predator told me; he chose me as his victim so that he could feel powerful because a villain was doing to him what he was doing to me. Revenge or power seeking at someone else's expense is never right. If your boss yelled at you because his boss yelled at him, would you say, "Oh it is ok, he is just blowing off some steam?" Once maybe, but regularly? "No;" the answer is "Yes" if you are still allowing people to victimize you.

I had a hard time with the Bible at first. The stuff the Bible talked about was so different from what I had experienced in my life. But once I started reading it more and putting it to the test, I found it to be true. My dysfunctional relationships decreased, and new healthy ones came into my life. I experienced God's unconditional love through people. I saw how people laid down their lives for me by helping me when I was at my lowest points. They even helped me when I thought I did not need help, but later I was so glad they did. I was very self-reliant and prideful. The following scenario was me at certain times in my life. It is like walking down the street texting, and someone grabs you, and you get mad only to find out later that they just saved you from getting hit by a car. This instant reaction of not trying to understand the situation first will continually be a stumbling block in life if healing is not your course of action.

Before I had safe people in my life, I was surrounded by people who only wanted to deal with me when I was happy. I had other "so-called friends" that did not care to hear about how I felt. Friends I had known for years would disappear during the hard times. But once I studied the Bible and started healing through my past, I found people who would ask me how I felt and what I wanted. I never was asked this in my family. Now I use a journal, or I talk it out with God in prayer. Yes, my friends are still willing to listen to me, and they do, but they are not my counselors. I found that because my family never listened to me longer than fifteen minutes, that having someone to listen to me and provide constructive feedback was terrific!

The women in the church started giving me books to help me understand and deal with my past traumas and encouraging me to seek professional help. At that time, I went to Christian Counseling Center which kept me rooted in my faith (even though the counselor did not go to the same church or might not have been the same denomination), she helped me face the horrors of my past and renewed my thinking so that I could function outside of continual counseling. Through the Bible, I learned what real love looked like, not just romantic love, but friendship love, family love, and neighborly love.

God is the only one that knows everything and why the abusers did what they did. He is the only one that can heal us because the "why" does not soothe us, and even the villain going to jail or dying does not relieve our pain. It takes time, prayers and tears and remembering the pain to bring healing. I know that God used certain occasions to expose me to new therapies and so when I hear about something, I keep an open mind to try it. It is usually perfect timing. God uses others to work the good for us.

A person must get those trapped feelings out. If they do not dig, they will experience more pain by repeating patterns or pushing away the people who love them or by being victimized in new and more painful ways. That unhealed pain will always be coming up, and the person will feel like life is full of pain, but if they face it, they will get through it. They will start to express new feelings of joy, peace, and excitement for life and grow in trust.

You must have a plan of how you will deal with your pain when it comes up. I went through years of both of my parents being very sick at the same time, and then they died three months apart from one another. During the holidays, birthdays and anniversaries were my most challenging times, and I would crave a drink. You must understand, all my life I never drank more than a half a wine cooler, and I can count on one hand the times in my life I drank before these deaths occurred.

But for a while, I wanted alcohol more often, and as time went by, the drinks got stronger. It started with a glass of wine and in a few months or even a year later, I was drinking a Long Island Ice Tea. I started ordering every drink I had ever overheard my friends order during my college years. Good thing the list was small. I have never been one to drink too much, but I was a lightweight, so half a wine cooler could do me in, and I was drinking mixed drinks by the end of that year.

If I had not put together a game plan of what I would do when I was missing my deceased parents, my sister, my grandparents, my aunts, my dogs, and too soon after that my late husband this could have been my life. Over time, this behavior could have turned my life upside down because of liver damage or a loss of my license due to drunk driving or a destroyed career or a failed marriage or a decrease in brain cells.

I have known people who had a bright future going for them and drinking lead to drugs and drugs lead to violence, and before the person knew it, they were in jail more often than they were out of jail. I know people who have good jobs that drink before work, at lunch, after work and on the weekends, but eventually, it catches up to them. They are running from something that is haunting them day and night. Can you relate?

Before I was unable to handle silence because my thoughts would overwhelm me. I had no answers to the questions that plagued me. I was too afraid to ask anyone else for answers because they might want to know why I needed to know. When I did start asking questions, no one had the answers, so I came up with this:

You may say, "I don't have a problem the predator does." Well, in life we have two choices when something terrible happens to us, we can choose to forgive, or we can decide to become bitter. I used to feel like my life was ruined because of what certain people did to me or how my family did not protect me. Then I started to exam my part in everything. You can either run from your pain, and it eventually catches up to you, or you can go after resolving it. I created this healing process. It helped me to work through years of pain in my life.

1.   I look at what the other person did to me that hurt me. What did they say or do that bothered me or not do that I needed from them? Was it on purpose or a mistake; did they repeat the offense even after apologizing? When they apologized, did they sincerely seem sorry? Did they show they did not care? Did they blame me for the way they behaved?

2.   At that time, how did that make me feel? What emotions did it stir up in me?

3.   When the situation occurred how did I choose to respond? How did it change my thinking, my behavior, my heart, and my relationships?

Note: I often look up scriptures that speak to the pain that was caused, to help me from spiraling into blame and bitterness. I also look up scriptures to redirect my reactions so I will not be self-righteous. I can then compare their sin and my sin with the scriptures so I can see no one was better than the other person because we both did not take the right path. This exercise exposes where change and growth are needed for all the parties involved.

Let's take a light scenario.

1.   Person X stole my money from my piggy bank. I needed her to appreciate our new friendship and be worthy of my mother and I's kindness.

"Do not **steal**. Do not lie. Do not deceive one another." Leviticus 19:11 New International Version (NIV)

2.   I felt hurt, sad, angry and distrustful.

"In your **anger** do not sin: Do not let the sun go down while you are still angry..." Ephesians 4:26 New International Version (NIV)

Jennifer Gamboa

3.   I responded by no longer saving money. I spent money as soon as I got it, so no one else could take it from me. This fear of having extra cash lying around caused me to buy things I did not need. It caused me to put my future at risk. It caused me not to have money for emergencies when I became an adult which resulted in me living paycheck to paycheck. I became an emotional spender. So, who has the problem, Person X or me?

It was something I pushed down, so I was reacting not even knowing why I was behaving this way until I started to dig. There are many things I began to push down to avoid hurt or shame. Then my reactions became extreme when I could not hold them down any longer. These responses caused me to feel embarrassed and shameful all over again. This pattern progressed since childhood causing me to have a festering volcano within me.

I cultivated anger as my instrument of protection, which was supposed to guard me against future hurt. It might have made me feel stronger than being afraid, but it hurt others around me. Hardship befalling others was not my intention. I had to change, or I would destroy healthy relationships with everyone around me.

I became selfish, emotionally indulgent, and distrusting of everyone. I was prideful because I only looked at how others hurt me and not how I hurt others. Usually, if I hurt specific people, I felt justified because it was payback for how they caused me anguish. I was slowly becoming a wrongdoer disregarding how I hurt people. If God did not intervene, I could have become a brute beast.

"A curse on **their uncontrolled anger**, on their indiscriminate wrath...." Genesis 49:7 The Message (MSG)

Here was a better way for me to respond since I knew God at least more than she did.

"Don't owe anything to anyone, except your outstanding debt to **continually love one another**, for the one who learns to love has fulfilled every requirement of the law." Romans 13:8 The Passion Translation (TPT)

Luckily, through finding God, my life began to heal. I make a daily effort to work my hurts out right away and go into the discussion with that person not thinking that they tried to hurt me on purpose. If I thought, they did whatever affliction against me by design, I would never be vulnerable enough to let them know how much anguish they caused me. Sometimes, I would get offended because something they said reminded me of something from my past that I had not resolved. Therefore, it was not their problem but mine. If you don't dig, you will continue to think it is the other person's problem.

When you realize it is your problem, you empower yourself to fix the problem. Why? For the single fact that you are in control of what you think, and say, and your actions. If you start caring enough to pay attention to what you feel and what you believe, you will draw healthy people to you that will value how you feel and want to know what you think. Then you will feel the love you thought was not there. The most valuable love starts with loving yourself for who you are (flaws and all).

CHAPTER THREE

WHAT IFs

"Your insight and understanding will protect you and prevent you from doing the wrong thing. **They will keep you away from people who stir up trouble** by what they say – those who have abandoned a righteous life to **live in the darkness** of sin, **those who find pleasure in doing wrong and who enjoy senseless evil**." Proverbs 2:11-14 Good News Translation (GNT)

The following is a story of how Jonadab stirred up trouble for his family by condoning Amnon's dark impulses.

No matter how much wealth you have and how much culture and training you have been exposed to, it does not protect you from evil. Let's look at a story.

"David's son Absalom had a beautiful unmarried sister named Tamar. Amnon, another of David's sons, fell in love with her. He was so much in love with her that he became sick because it seemed impossible for him to have her; as a virgin, she was kept from meeting men. But he had a friend, a very shrewd man named Jonadab, the son of David's brother Shammah. Jonadab said to Amnon, "You are the king's son, yet day after day I see you looking sad. What's the matter?" "I'm in love with Tamar, the sister of my half-brother Absalom," he answered."

"Jonadab said to him, "Pretend that you are sick and go to bed. When your father comes to see you, say to him, "Please ask my sister Tamar to come and feed me. I want her to fix the food here where I can see her, and then serve it to me herself." So Amnon pretended that he was sick and went to bed.""

"King David went to see him, and Amnon said to him, "Please let Tamar come and make a few cakes here where I can see her, and then serve them to me herself.""

"So, David sent word to Tamar in the palace: "Go to Amnon's house and fix him some food." She went there and found him in bed. She took some dough, prepared it, and made some cakes there where he could see her. Then she baked the cakes and emptied them out of the pan for him to eat, but he wouldn't. He said, "Send everyone away"- and they all left. Then he said to her, "Bring the cakes here to my bed and serve them to me yourself." She took the cakes and went over to him. As she offered them to him, he grabbed her and said, "Come to bed with me!"

"No," she said. "Don't force me to do such a degrading thing! That's awful! How could I ever hold up my head in public again? And you - you would be completely disgraced in Israel. Please, speak to the king, and I'm sure that he will give me to you." But he would not listen to her, and since he was stronger than she was, he overpowered her and raped her."

"Then Amnon was filled with a deep hatred for her; he hated her now even more than he had loved her before. He said to her, "Get out!" "No," she answered. "To send me away like this is a greater crime than what you just did!" "But Amnon would not listen to her; he called in his personal servant and said, "Get this woman out of my sight! Throw her out and lock the door!" The servant put her out and locked the door.

Jennifer Gamboa

Tamar was wearing a long robe with full sleeves, the usual clothing for an unmarried princess in those days. She sprinkled ashes on her head, tore her robe, and with her face buried in her hands went away crying. When her brother Absalom saw her, he asked, "Has Amnon molested you? Please sister, don't let it upset you so much. He is your half-brother, so don't tell anyone about it." So, Tamar lived in Absalom's house sad and lonely."

"When King David heard what had happened, he was furious. And Absalom hated Amnon so much for having raped his sister Tamar that he would no longer even speak to him." 2 Samuel 13:1-22 Good News Translation (GNT)

I am going to jump ahead into the story years later.

"David was told: Absalom has killed all your sons – not one of them is left!" The king stood up, tore his clothes in sorrow, and threw himself to the ground. The servants who were there with him tore their clothes also. But Jonadab, the son of David's brother Shammah, said, "Your Majesty, they haven't killed all your sons. Only Amnon is dead. You could tell by looking at Absalom that he had made up his mind to do this from the time that Amnon raped his sister Tamar. So, don't believe the news that all your sons are dead; only Amnon was killed. Absalom fled … and stayed away three years." 2 Samuel 13:30-33, 37 Good News Translation (GNT)

The sad thing is even in this story it proves true that when the predator is held accountable for his crimes it does not heal the collateral damage to that person or the other people involved in that person's life. From the day Amnon was killed, Tamar did not move out of her brother's house, nor did she get married or live happily ever after. Her brother defended her honor, but she lost him in the end. You don't hear about her family rallying around her to provide her support. Quite often others want to sweep challenging things under the rug. They expect you to move on with your life because they have no idea what else to tell you to do. Her sadness and shame remained.

It is up to us to write a different story for our lives. We must start and finish the healing process whether the criminal is brought to justice or not. The more of us who heal, the more we will give hope to the countless others that these various crimes have impacted.

Absalom was so full of anger and sadness for his sister that he decided to move from feelings of helplessness and hopelessness to taking matters into his own hands by committing murder. He was not only enraged by Amnon's actions, but he was angry at his dad for not doing more to seek justice for Tamar. His anger is revealed later in the story when Absalom returns to his father's kingdom and turns as many people against King David as possible before overthrowing him as the King. His actions are an effort to make himself feel better. Absalom was going through his inner-turmoil; he lost sight of what his sister needed to be able to heal and move on with her own life.

The definition of rape was revised in the following way, "Rapes (legacy definition from 80 years ago) increased 4.4 percent and rapes (revised definition from 2012) rose 3.5 percent in 2016." What was in the category of rape needed to be revised to include more cases that were being reported. "The FBI's UCR Program initiated a revised definition within the Summary Based Reporting System in 2013. The term "forcible" was removed from the offense name, and the definition was changed to "penetration, no matter how slight, of the vagina or anus with any body part or object, or oral penetration by a sex organ of another person, without the consent of the victim. Of the 18,415 agencies that reported to the UCR this year, 10,000 of them are using the revised definition of rape." "The numbers of sex offenses reflected in the UCR program could increase by more than 40 percent but it still excludes statutory rape," based on the newspaper article from XX Factor called The FBI Finally Ditches Its 80-Year-Old Definition of Rape by Amanda Hess dated 11/10/2014. "Based on the new definition of rape there were 135,755 rapes reported to law enforcement" from Homeland Security Today in an article called FBI's 2017 Crime Statistics Show Decreases in Violent and Property Crimes dated 9/24/18. Rapes that happen on college campuses that are reported to the college are not included in these statistics. 95% of college rapes are never reported to authorities.

Until you start digging, you don't know what is really important to you. I thought avoiding pain was the most important thing to me. But once I dug and wrote and talked, I realized SAFETY was the most important thing to me. When people go after healing, they will feel anger and relive the powerlessness, but then they will also feel powerful and safer. Just feeling "safe" or "powerful" is enough to start the journey, I think. I remember the first time I felt safe as an adult. It made me cry because I realized I had never felt that way before. This emotion was not a "sadness or suffering" outpouring of tears, but it was droplets of joy which was unfamiliar to me. Remember happiness is different than momentary pleasure or fun or the excitement of a party.

You will have to learn to forgive yourself. Again, it was not your fault whether you were a child or a grownup, but we all have these "what-ifs" that plague our minds. We as humans need to stop second-guessing ourselves. Sometimes we are just in the wrong place at the wrong time. Sometimes we just get fooled by a charismatic psychopath.

Let's run through some of the what-ifs that keep us stuck – it is what I call, "Believing the Lies" we have fallen for; the villains' mind tricks that told us it was our fault instead of the villain's fault.

Sexual Abuse (Rape & Molestation)

"I should have screamed."

"I should have fought harder."

"Maybe, I should not have fought back. It just made the person madder."

"I should have never gone to that party."

"I should have never parked so far away."

"I should have never gotten in that car."

51

"I should have run."

"I should not have worn those high heels."

"I should have never drunk that much alcohol."

"I should not have used that drug."

"I should have never ignored the warning feeling that I felt."

"I should have known better."

"I should have never trusted that person."

"What did I do to deserve this?"

"What is wrong with me that I got molested or raped by someone of the same gender?"

"What did I do that made them chose me?"

"I was a young boy; why did I not enjoy being touched, kissed by an older woman – isn't that every man's fantasy?"

"Can people look at me and see I am damaged?"

"Why did my husband force himself on me? I thought he loved me. He could have just asked or romanced me or waited."

"Why did my mom allow those men to have sex with my little sister?"

No matter what a person does, they will second guess themselves. Did you do the right thing? Is there anything you could have done differently that would have made the situation turn in your favor? When you answer these questions, ask if your answers are accurate. Then ask again are they really true. The other important question to ask yourself is how would I feel if I did not believe this, and how would I act differently?

There is no 100% wins in life. One day you will be at the wrong place at the wrong time. Or you will be weak or sick or tired. You could also have a power day where you feel the strongest you have ever been, healthy and fit and someone will still be faster, stronger or catch you off your guard. Some people have so much charisma, or are so polished or are so talented at fooling people that you would never suspect them as the perpetrator, but they are, and they gain your trust and get the upper hand. Maybe, you can learn from it, but the lesson is not to never trust again.

"An estimated 17.7 million American women had been the prey of attempted or completed rape since crime began being reported until the year 1998," based on National Institute of Justice ... Violence Against Women Survey dated 1998. "Every 98 seconds a sexual assault happens in America. On average, there are 321,500 casualties age 12 or older of rape and sexual assault each year in the United States," based on the Department of Justice... Statistics, National Crime Victimization Survey, 2012-2016 dated 2017.

"The USA has an estimated population of 327,000,000 people, and it is the top country with the highest rape occurrences in the world. As of 2015, rape in the United States of America was 124,047 cases; that accounts for 52.93% of the world's rape crimes. The world's total reported rapes were estimated at 234,354 in 2015. The top 5 countries other than the USA are Mexico, Colombia, France, and Peru accounting for 74.90 % of it based on Crime-Statistics on Sexual-Rape."

I had seven years of martial arts, and the attempted rapist also had advanced martial arts skills. All I remember was seeing the sky and then the grass over and over. After I was able to slip out from the position, he had me pinned in, he just stopped the heinous act and disappeared as quickly as he had shown up.

"The average number of rape cases reported in the US annually is 89,000. Sadly, 60% of rapes are never reported to authorities. Ages 12-34 are the highest risk years for statutory rape and sexual assault; 15% of the victims are age 12-17, 54% of the victims are age 18-34. 28% of the victims are age 35-64, and 3% are over the age of 65," based on a report from Rainn titled Victims of Sexual Violence statistics titled Younger People Are at the Highest Risk of Sexual Violence.

"One out of six American women were targets of attempted or completed rape in her lifetime. 92% of sexual assaults were committed against females. 47% of these crimes involved both victim and perpetrator; both had been drinking. 38% of people were raped by a friend or acquaintance. 26% of the females were assaulted by a stranger. 7% were sexually abused by a relative. 28% of this group were raped by "an intimate" (dating, boyfriend, fiancée, husband). 31% were raped in the perpetrators home, and 27% were raped in the victims' home. 7% were raped at a party, 7% were violated in a vehicle, 4% were defiled outdoors, and 2% were raped in a bar," based on National Institute of Justice...& Consequences of Violence Against Women Survey dated 1998.

"Men and Boys are also affected by sexual violence. 2.78 million men in the United States have been victims of attempted or completed rape. One out of every ten rape targets are males. One in thirty-three males has experienced an attempted or completed rape in their lifetime. 3% of men experienced an attempted or completed rape," based on the National Institute of Justice & Centers for Disease Control & Prevention. 21% of TGQN (transgender, genderqueer, nonconforming) college students have been sexually assaulted, compared to 18% of non-TGQN females, and 4% of non-TGQN males," based on the Association of American Universities (AAU), Report on the AAU Campus Climate Survey on Sexual Assault and Sexual Misconduct dated September 21, 2015.

"Sexual assault is a major concern in India. More than 33,000 rapes were reported in 2014. The rate of these assaults is increasing. Rape is one of India's most common crimes against women. 24,923 rape cases were reported across India in 2012, but experts agree that the number of unreported cases of sexual assault brings the total much higher. The latest estimates suggest that a new case of rape is reported every 22 minutes in India," according to the National Crime Records Bureau.

South Africa also has one of the highest rates of rape in the world. AIDS also is a concern there, and it has been reported that if a woman is raped, there is a 25% chance her attacker has HIV or AIDS.

"**They will be paid with suffering for the suffering they have caused.**" 2 Peter 2:13 Good News Translation (GNT)

The aftermath effects of sexual assaults on people report, "Sexual violence affects the person's relationships with their family, friends, and co-workers. 38% of people of sexual violence experience work or school problems, which can include significant issues with a boss, coworker, or peer. 37% experience family or friend problems, including getting into arguments more frequently than before, not feeling able to trust their family or friends, or not being emotionally as close to them as before the crime. 84% of people who pulled through the attack were violated by an intimate partner; 79% of people who endured the offense were victimized by a family member, close friend or acquaintance. 67% of people who withstood the attack by a stranger all victims experience professional or emotional issues, including moderate to severe distress, or increased problems at work or school." based on a Rainn report researched from Department of Justice, Office of Justice Programs, Bureau of Justice Statistics, Socio-emotional Impact of Violent Crime dated 2014.

You don't have to be a statistic. You can be the exception to the rule. Here are some scriptures to give you hope and guidance.

"Jesus looked at them and said, "**With man this is impossible, but with God all things are possible.**" Matthew 19:26 New International Version (NIV)

"Not so, my lord," Hannah replied, "**I am a woman who is deeply troubled**. I have not been drinking wine or beer; **I was pouring out my soul to the Lord.**" 1 Samuel 1:15 New International Version (NIV)

Be the one that overcomes no matter what the odds are! You have a choice. You are in control. You are stronger than you think.

The effects of this crime can be overwhelming, but there is an excellent treatment that will bring relief and healing called EMDR. In Chapter Six, I will go into more details about it. I really like EMDR (Eye Movement Desensitization Reprocessing), it is faster than conventional therapy. There are also audiobooks and paperback books that will give you strategies in case you don't have the money or time to go to treatment, but eventually going to an EMDR professional will work to your advantage because if they see you getting stuck or getting too emotional, they can redirect you. Every few sessions you work through a significant life event and leave resolved. I have found this to work tremendously well for people with Post Traumatic Syndrome no matter what the cause of the trauma.

"How enriched are they who find their strength in the Lord; within their hearts are the highways of holiness! **Even when their paths wind through the dark valley of tears, they dig deep to find a pleasant pool where others find only pain. He gives to them a brook of blessing filled from the rain of an outpouring.**" Psalm 84:5-6 The Passion Translation (TPT)

Suicide is a terrible long-term solution for a temporary problem. No problem lasts forever; even chronic conditions go into remission, or you have your good days. No one wants their story to end with such tragedy. That is the purpose of grace, mercy, and forgiveness. There is nothing that cannot be healed through the miraculous power of our Creator. Love yourself enough to Never Give Up! The Angels in heaven are rooting for you. You are worth it. You are here for a reason.

I have spent the last twenty-one years of my life talking to and sharing with women and men who had tragedies in their lives offering hope and reading material, scriptures, and prayer to all who would listen. I have seen many lives change through going after discovering what is causing them discomfort, instead of denying it and running away.

Some of you may not be at the point in your life where you care about your future or your life. That can change. I know people who used to wait to die and nothing mattered to them. They lived a robotic existence. But after seeking help and turning around their relationships, they look forward to their future. They love their life. They are happy and not ruled by fear. They like others, not just those people who give to them.

CHAPTER FOUR

THE BLAME GAME

Then we have the other side where we blame God or others.

Physical Abuse (Bullying)

"If God deals out justice, why has my mom been beaten by my dad even after the police have come to our home several times?"

"Why can't God stop my dad from drinking, then he would not beat me?"

"Why did they have to beat me within an inch of me losing my life for a gold watch? Why didn't my friends help me?

"Why did they have to kick me and break my ribs over some Timberland shoes?"

"Why did they have to embarrass me in front of the whole class? I cannot help that I stutter. Why did God create me to stutter? Why did God create mean kids?"

"Why did they have to push me around in front of the girl that I liked? Why did God make me short or chubby or albino or have a learning disability?"

"I don't bother anyone. Why do they have to pick on me in the locker room? Why do they have to put the video of them bullying me on the Internet? Why did God create the Internet to be used in such an evil way?"

"How can I trust him after he smacks me around and then he cries and brings me flowers and promises he will stop drinking or won't do it again? But it is not long before he forgets every single promise and every tear has dried up, and I see his fist flying toward my stomach or knocks me off my feet from a blow to my head I did not even see coming. Where did all that love go? Does true love exist?"

"He has me by the throat with his one arm, while the rest of my body dangles from the corner of the ceiling. I have no idea what set him off today. I am so tired of being afraid of him."

"When your heart overflows with understanding you'll be very slow to get angry. **But if you have a quick temper, your impatience will be quickly seen by all.**" Proverbs 14:29 The Passion Translation (TPT)

If it is your dad or mom is abusing you, and the other parent is an enabler or codependent or passive bystander, then go to someone else who is protective and strong, and willing to stand up for what is right. If you are being abused or bullied by a student tell a teacher you trust or the principal or counselor. Do not give up! Do whatever you have to do to get the person to stop hurting you without hurting yourself or ending your life. There are no take backs in **Death. It is a permanent solution to a temporary problem.** I know when you are going through something fierce, it is like time slows down. It feels like this is never going to end.

Suicide does not hurt the people who hurt you. They are devoid of compassion, guilt or normal healthy emotions. It only hurts and confuses the people who love you. They cannot take over your "cause" because you are not there to answer the questions. Please do not run away; this makes you exposed to many different predators. If you can find a safe relative to move in with that would be better, but you will have to file a report so your parents cannot just come and take you home.

"Wine is a mocker and beer a brawler; whoever is led astray by them is not wise." Proverbs 20:1 New International Version (NIV)

"The world's definition of assault – 'Assault' means a physical attack against the body of another person resulting in serious bodily injury, excluding indecent, sexual assault, threats, and slapping or punching. 'Assault' leading to death should also be excluded. A person is guilty of aggravated assault if he or she attempts to cause serious bodily injury to another or causes such injury purposely, knowingly, or recklessly under the circumstances manifesting extreme indifference to the value of human life, or attempts to cause or purposely or knowingly causes bodily injury to another with a deadly weapon. In all jurisdiction's statutes punish such aggravated assaults as assault with intent to murder (or rob or kill or rape) and assault with a dangerous (or deadly) weapon more severely than "simple" assaults.

According to the January 9, 2017, article FBI Releases Preliminary Semiannual Crime Statistics for 2016 says "On average, nearly 20 people per minute are physically abused by an intimate partner in the United States. During one year, this equates to more than 10 million women and men. 1 in 3 women and 1 in 4 men have been the prey of physical violence by an intimate partner. 1 in 4 women and 1 in 7 men have been the scapegoat of severe physical violence by an intimate partner in their lifetime. 1 in 7 women and 1 in 18 men have been stalked to the point in which they felt very fearful or believed that they or someone close to them would be harmed or killed by an intimate partner. On a typical day, there are more than 20,000 phone calls placed to domestic violence hotlines nationwide."

"In Pakistan, domestic violence occurs in forms of beatings, sexual violence, torture, mutilation, acid attacks and burning the victim alive (bride burning). A 2011 report claims 80% of women in Pakistan suffer from domestic abuse. A 2004 study claimed 50% of the women in Pakistan are physically battered, and 90% of women are mentally and verbally abused by their men; other reports claim domestic violence rates between 70% to over 95% in Pakistan" based on the findings of Nation Master.

"In Hong Kong instances of indecent assault rose by 5.7% to 1,077 reports in 2017" based on Hong Kong Law & Crime.

"Domestic victimization is correlated with a higher rate of depression and suicidal behavior. Intimate partner violence accounts for 15% of all violent crimes. It is common for women between the ages of 18-24 to be abused by an intimate partner. Only 34% of people who are injured by intimate partners receive medical care for their injuries. 19% of domestic violence involves a weapon. The presence of a gun in a domestic violence situation increases the risk of homicide by 500%."

"If anyone causes one of these little ones - those who believe in me - to stumble, it would be better

for them if a large millstone were hung around their neck and they were thrown into the sea." 2 Peter 2:22 New International Version (NIV)

The effects on the bullied individual can include social isolation, shame, sleep disturbance, changes in eating habits, low self-esteem, school avoidance, poor school performance, anxiety, bedwetting, depression, higher risk of illness, and stomachaches, headaches, muscle aches, and other physical complaints with no known medical cause.

It is terrible when a child cannot get a good education because they are so anxious and afraid of their peers that they will encounter on the way to school or once they arrive at school. It is even sadder when there is no peace in their home. Or a child cannot enjoy his or her vacation with the family because the siblings or cousins are nice in front of the parents, but are cruel once they are out of the grownups sight.

Since the physically abused person will develop conditions that will cause a lot of physical problems in the future, besides the immediate pain, I recommend Neuro Emotional Technique (NET). Please understand that you need to get away from the violence that is being acted out on you, and once you do, NET will restore your body to a much healthier state than physical therapy or living on pain medicines. It is a combination of chiropractic treatment, and when necessary it includes unique homeopathic remedies to support the body's natural healing process. NET is used for healing the pain that comes from stress, past trauma, and current events.

Unlike most treatments, you can do it without having to tell the doctor your problems. Somethings are so horrible you are unable to speak them aloud so this works for that. You think it, and then the doctor taps on certain spots on your back while you apply pressure to other places on your body that he or she instructs you to press on. This relieves the pain in minutes, and it stays gone for months.

I had neck, shoulder and back pain that would last for three weeks non-stop and I had been to other chiropractors for seven years at a time going in several times a week. It would help for a couple of days, and then the pain would come back, but with a combination of chiropractic treatment and NET, it stays away for six months or longer. I forgot what it felt like to be able to get a good night's sleep and be without pain every day; with no more pain, my joy returned.

I know many people who have been treated with NET, and we all believe it is incredible! I have never even had to take any homeopathic remedies. The NET treatment is done on me before the doctor does any chiropractic treatment, so I know it is the NET that is working. Scott Walker who invented NET graduated from Palmer College of Chiropractic, so when you look for treatment, you will have to look up chiropractors. I have been to four different types of chiropractors in the last thirty years, and NET is the best. This kind of treatment works for anxiety or stress. In Chapter Six, I will go into more detail about how it works.

Kidnapping

"Why did God allow me to get kidnapped?"

"I should have screamed louder."
"I should have never worn flip-flops. Maybe, I would have been able to get away."
"Why can't I see my mommy?"
"When can I go home?"
"Why are you doing this?"
"Why can't I go to school? I miss my friends."

Even a kidnapped person ends up believing the kidnappers lies. The victim complies to the kidnapper in order to be to feed and kept alive. Some people are held for ten and twenty years, and something false becomes their reality; maybe that is the victims' survival method.

"The total abductions in 2002 are 797,500. The causes and categories the USA has for children going missing are: 43.2% of people are runaways or throwaways; 41% are benign explanations; 7.5% are missing involuntarily, lost or injured; 6.8% are family abductions; 1.5% are non-family abductions. 35% of children abducted are 6-11 years of age; 23% of children abducted are age 3-5 years old; 21% of children abducted are age 0-2 years old; 17% of children abducted are age 12-14 years old; 4% of children abducted are age 15-17 years old; 53% of the children are abducted by their fathers," based on a report from RAINN.

Despite representing 12.85% of the USA population, 270,000 minorities have gone missing since 2010. Black Americans accounted for nearly 226,000 or 34% of all missing persons reported in 2012 according to the Atlanta Black Star.

"Germany is the top country in the world in kidnapping crimes. As of 2015, kidnapping incidents in Germany reached 4,789 per 100,000 population. That accounts for 21.74 % of the world's kidnappings. The top 5 countries (other than Germany) are France, Canada, Mexico, and Belgium accounting for 66.43% of it. The world's total kidnappings were estimated at 22,025 in 2015. France had 3,985 kidnappings in 2015. For Canada, 3,555 kidnappings happened in 2015. Belgium had 1,143 kidnapping occurring in 2015. Kidnapping has surged in Mexico since 2005 by gangs to get ransoms. Mexico had 1,160 kidnappings during 2015, and nearly 1,200 kidnappings occurred in Mexico in 2017," according to data from the Mexican National System of Public Security (NSPS).

Hostage and kidnap victims can experience stress which will show up in their thinking, emotions, and interactions. They may feel shock, numbness, helplessness, anxiety, guilt, depression, and anger. They could experience continual replaying of the events in their mind or denial, impaired memory, decreased concentration, being overly cautious and aware, confusion or fear of the ordeal happening again. They will tend to be on edge and withdraw from family, friends, and activities. They will need time to adjust back into family or work.

When hostages are released, it is essential for them to receive medical attention right away. They need to be in a safe and secure environment. It is vital for them to connect with emotionally healthy loved ones. Protect their privacy by avoiding media overexposure including watching and listening to the news and participating in media interviews. They should be encouraged to talk when they are ready and journal until then, so their experiences don't keep replaying in their heads. Provide them with many alternatives for treatment and let them choose the counseling that speaks to them. It is like a "Knowing" when you hear it, you will know deep down inside that the information or treatment is for you. For some of us, it is that which we want to do the least that will help us the most. You can show them little clips of the type of therapy so they can have an idea of what to expect. This will make it easier to choose instead of only seeing a list of available treatments. You can help with the decisions because they will probably still be in shock or overwhelmed.

Problems in Marriage

"What did I do wrong? I was a good wife! Why did my husband leave me for a man?"

"I kept the house clean. I never let him see me without makeup. I always tried to look my best and keep our sex life exciting. Why did he have an affair?"

"Why did God give me a husband that is unfaithful to me and caused me to get an STD that eventually turned to cancer?"

"Why doesn't my husband take me on dates anymore?"

"Why doesn't my husband help me with the kids or the housework?"

"Why is my husband always out with his friends? He spends more time with them than at home, and I feel so lonely."

"Why does my wife always complain? It makes me feel like I can never do anything right."

"Why doesn't my wife ever say, "please" or "thank you?" She only supplies me her "Honey to Do List" or barks commands. I feel like I am married to my mother!"

"Why does my time with my wife always involve her family? I feel like I am married to her family instead of her."

"Maybe, I married too young. I should have dated more to see what was out there. I married my first boyfriend, and I feel like that was a mistake because he is not financially responsible. Some utility is always being cut off due to lack of payment. If I did not save the day, our car would have been repossessed. I thought the man was supposed to provide for his family! Will I ever have that life?"

"I don't want to get a divorce, but I cannot continue to live like this. I feel his drinking is destroying us!"

"He went on: "It's what comes out of a person that pollutes: obscenities, lusts, thefts, murders, adulteries, greed, depravity, deceptive dealings, carousing, mean looks, slander, arrogance, foolishness—all these are vomit from the heart. *There* is the source of your pollution." Mark 7:20-23 The Message (MSG)

You might be the person that never says, "No." If you do, it is usually after months or years of working through this issue or some experience that shakes you so much you cannot remain the same. The problem could be you are an enabler, you are codependent, or you have very weak boundaries. No matter if you are perfect; an unfaithful person will find an excuse to cheat. It is about them trying to fill a bottomless pit that cannot be filled; it has to be healed. The root is not feeling loved or not knowing how to say, "No" or a lack of self-control or just selfishness or repeating patterns seen in the childhood family dynamic. If you are always there when he gets home to wait on him, you are teaching him it is ok to take you for granted. Get your own life, and he may start missing you.

It is not up to you to try to heal him. It is up to you to stand up for yourself and show others how to treat you with respect by you showing respect for yourself and using your strength to create a happy life for yourself. If your husband leaves you at home all the time, go out with friends while he is out. Join a group doing some favorite hobbies you always wanted to explore. Go back to school to get a degree or get certified to become more valuable in your career. Love yourself.

Do something constructive with your time. Don't go out and spend money you don't have or use up your emergency money. Don't start drinking or have an affair. Be the better person. If the dysfunctional person walks away from you, it may hurt, but it will be a blessing in disguise. Understand you deserve better! Heal and grow before starting a new relationship, or you might find yourself in the same kind of partnership, only he or she has a different name.

If you want to learn to change your marriage the book "The Heart of the Five Love Languages" by Gary Chapman is very informative and helpful. Love languages focus on what is essential to the other person in order to strengthen the relationship. You try to love your partner in the way that makes you feel loved, but you get hurt when they are not receiving your love messages. It is because your love language isn't your partner's love language. You have to learn their love language, so you can fill their love tank because once it is empty that is what leads to divorce. Examples of love languages are physical touch, receiving gifts, words of affirmation, and quality time. If your wife is into quality time, you will need to make sure you are there for all the significant events in her life, the birth of your children, substantial illnesses, deaths in the family, birthdays, holidays and anniversaries, etc.

If your husband's love language is quality time watch his favorite sports team with him on TV, or surprise him with tickets to a game. Do something he likes to do that you might not like for no other reason than to please him.

If your partner is into physical touch don't just wait to touch her when you want to have sex. Give her hugs often and kiss her, put your hand on her hand or rub her back, these small gestures will mean the world to her. If you are not an affectionate person, you will have to learn.

If your partner needs words of affirmation, praise your husband when he cooks for you, or plays with the kids or picks up the dry cleaning. Compliment him on his body, or clothes or features you especially like, thank him for cleaning your car, or fixing the car or repairing the sink or driving you around. Compliment him when he does things that encourage you; this will cause him to do more of those things rather than when you complain about what you don't like. You can also write him a card or a love letter or leave him special notes of appreciation regularly.

If your wife is into receiving gifts, you could buy her flowers, learn what her favorite flowers are so it will mean more. Go shopping with her and see what she likes and go back later and buy it for her and surprise her with it on a different day.

Stereotypical gender roles need to be discussed. Even if your wife is a stay at home mom, ask her if she needs any help with the dishes or preparing dinner or getting the kids ready for bed and draw her a bath so she can soak and relax. Thank her often for the things you usually take for granted.

Another great book is "Men Are from Mars, Women Are from Venus" by John Gray. This book helps you to understand the mind of a woman and a man. This book explains things in great depth and is something you should practice and refer to often. It is unlike any other book I have ever read on the subject of relationships. We say simple words, but men and women get a totally different meaning from these words, and this is the reason for most of the arguments and frustrations.

Emotional & Psychological Abuse

"If God is perfect. Why did he give me this family?" (A question posed by the abused or devalued or abandoned or neglected.)

"Why couldn't my parents have money so I would not have to be in a neighborhood where I have to be chased by bullies every day."

"Why can't God have given me loving parents? I would not have to be in this foster home."

"Why does this world have to be this way – where I have to walk past people selling drugs or prostitutes soliciting to customers."

"Why did God put me in a single parent home? I should be coming home being nurtured and supported. But instead, I have been shoved into the role of the other absent parent, listening to mom's problems, comforting her, being her friend, and taking on adult responsibilities. I had to start working at a young age to help out at home. Don't I deserve to be a kid?"

"He called me stupid again. Maybe, I would be able to get all good grades, if there was not so much pressure to get straight A's. I got a B+, and my world blows up, knowing that when I get home, I will get the speech about how I have destroyed my chances of getting into the best colleges, and that all my friends will leave me behind. When they come back to visit during the break, I will be taking their order at the drive-thru window at some fast food establishment! He continues to remind me how I am letting down the family legacy of Masters Degrees and PhDs. What a disappointment I am and why did I have to be his son!"

"I washed my clothes in hot water instead of cold water and my skirt shrank. My mom tells me I am going out of the house looking like a prostitute. I walked out before she finishes her statement about me ending up like my sister pregnant before graduating

73

from high school. Blah, Blah. I wish I could walk away from it, but her words finish in my head before I arrive at school. They cause me anxiety and lacerate my self-worth. Her negative words are like a recording; I cannot turn off. I cannot remember one good thing she has ever said about me that did not end in some insult."

"There goes my aunt again comparing me to my older brother, "Why can't you be more like Richard? Why are you so awkward? Maybe you should join the football team or some other sport and learn how to be coordinated! Maybe, then you could get a girlfriend. Why must you always hang out with those nerdy kids?" She continues with the 101 things wrong with me. I try to drown her out by rehearsing my speech in my head for my debate class this afternoon. I hear we choose our parents? Does that mean I chose the rest of my family members also?"

"Can you bridle your tongue when your heart is under pressure? That's how you show that you are wise. An understanding heart keeps you cool, calm, and collected, no matter what you're facing." Proverbs 17:27 The Passion Translation (TPT)

What these people say about you is not true. They are unhappy and want you to be the same. They use their words to release their anger or stress or worry. Maybe they see something in you that makes them feel inferior, so they try to shut you down to make themselves feel better about where they are in life because they are competitive. You cannot stop them from speaking, but you can label it a lie and throw it out with the trash. You have to remember the problem is theirs, not yours. Remember to try to avoid becoming like them to someone else. You can bully someone with your words.

"We all stumble in many ways. Anyone who is never at fault in what they say is perfect, able to keep their whole body in check. When we put bits into the mouths of horses to make them obey us, we can turn the whole animal. Or take ships as an example. Although they are so large and are driven by strong winds, they are steered by a very small rudder wherever the pilot wants to go. Likewise, the tongue is a small part of the body, but it makes great boasts. Consider what a great forest is set on fire by a small spark. The tongue also is a fire, a world of evil among the parts of the body. It corrupts the whole body, sets the whole course of one's life on fire, and is itself set on fire by hell. All kinds of animals, birds, reptiles and sea creatures are being tamed and have been tamed by mankind, but no human being can tame the tongue. It is a restless evil, full of deadly poison. With the tongue, we praise our Lord and Father, and with it, we curse human beings, who have been made in God's likeness. Out of the same mouth come praise and cursing. My brothers and sisters, this should not be." James 3:2-10 New International Version (NIV)

The issues in the marriage and emotional abuse sections would benefit from Grief Recovery treatment. It is a program that helps people deal with the loss of trust, loss of safety and loss of control over one's body plus other disappointments. It deals with the things that people say when they are trying to comfort you that do so much damage to you the person they love and want to help. It teaches you how to overcome these pep talks that would cause you to isolate. It deals with the loss of jobs, divorce, relationships, and death. I will go into more details about how it works in Chapter Six.

Betrayal, Broken Trust, Destroyed Livelihood

"Why did God not stop me from signing that business contract with those wolves in sheep's clothing? I worked for half my life to get where I am. They feel they deserve what I have and can come and steal it away from me! Why was I born into this competitive family?"

"Why! Why? I saved up my money since our kids were born and then my wife goes out and spends it on clothes she will only wear once or maybe never. Why do I save up for our kids for college only to have her burn through it in a weekend? Why didn't God make me listen to the red flags? Why cannot God get her under control? How do I tell our twins they cannot go to college because we have no money now?"

"I dedicated our whole marriage to raising our kids. I walked away from a great career to be a stay home mom to give him sons; and he decides to leave me for a younger woman. Then he keeps me in court until I have no money left. He had all the money and will always have more money than I have. I have to try to find a career. No a job! Who will hire someone who has been out of the workforce for 21 years? Where will I get the money to eat and where will I find a place that I can afford on an entry-level wage? I am already losing the house and the car. Now I will have to let go of most of my clothes because I have nowhere to store them. I have no money for a storage facility, and I have no relatives who live locally. I lost most of my friends because they are married and I am now single. What great sin did I do to deserve my world being annihilated?"

"Community Property State! It is my home, and I paid for it. How is that community property? Why should I have to sell my house because I am tired of all the pain and suffering my deadbeat husband puts me through. Now that I have enough backbone to say no more, I have to lose my home! I put everything into this house to make it a home for us. Why should he get half of the equity when I labored day in and day out to pay for it, clean it and remodel it? I won't have enough for 20% down on a new house. He is just going to drink, smoke or party his portion away. I thought laws were made to protect the innocent? He is a man; he will easily find some desperate, lonely woman he could move in with."

"I know what I'm doing. I have it all planned out - **plans to take care of you, not abandon you, plans to give you the future you hope for. When you call on me, when you come and pray to me, I'll listen.** "When you come looking for me, you'll find me. Yes, when you get serious about finding me and want it more than anything else, **I'll make sure you won't be disappointed.**" GOD's Decree. Jeremiah 29:12-14 The Message (MSG)

Don't think life is over because of a divorce. Now that you know what a cheater, liar, thief, abuser looks like you can avoid that kind of person in the future. You will be stronger for it. Once healed your path will be free and clear and you can pick out the rare jewels, diamonds, and keepsake in people. You won't fall for the pieces of glass or plastic or Cubic Zirconia thinking you have a diamond.

"You won't fall for fool's gold in place of the real thing as long as you work on yourself before you start a new relationship. If you don't learn from your mistakes, then we as humans tend to repeat them. Do you want a person with charisma or a good character? There is 25% real gold in fool's gold, but the 75% is something unknown, undesirable, and not what you expected. When you choose good character, then you get 100% gold. Charisma is like opening a beautifully wrapped present and finding nothing inside the box. After you work on yourself, you will be whole again or whole for the first time.

I waited a while to get married because I did not want to get divorced or worse be unhappily married for the rest of my life. My first husband hurt me more than combining all my past disappointments from my other previous relationships into one. I had to go on depression medicine for three months, but then I decided to detox and started fresh with tackling the problem head-on instead of putting a band aid on it and hoping it would heal.

I went to counseling for two years before I started my next relationship with Joseph. It was like I had waited my whole life for him, and the depth of our relationship could not compare to all the good in my past relationships combined. We did 158 firsts together. We lived life to the fullest. If I had not married that first man that caused me to need to go to counseling, which was something I hated doing because of the past bad experiences, I would not have recognized the value in Joseph. Counseling helped me break old patterns. I was a whole person. Joseph just complimented who I was becoming and facilitated me to reach higher levels than if I was still dating men from my old patterns.

I have found that even some of the most famous people use **Hypnosis** to help them to overcome their past issues. There are hypnosis audiobooks that are 30 minutes long so you can listen to it before you go to bed, which is best, or if and when you take a nap at lunch.

Affirmations are very useful for breaking old habits and changing poor thinking patterns. With affirmations, you need to know the format so that you understand how the mind works. You will fashion messages that work specifically on what you are dealing with in your life. Always use positive words, and ideas. Never use the actual word you are trying avoid for example: "Please don't let me fail this test." Or "I don't want to be heavy all my life." "Help me stop being lonely." The subconscious hears, "I want to be heavy all my life." "Please let me fail this test." "Help me be lonely." Use the opposite words. Do use words that show lack like "want," "need," "help." Use sentences with "I am" or "I have." "I am fit and trim." "I have passed the test with a high score." 'I am happy, and my life is full of love, and I share a wonderful companionship with a man who is my perfect mate." The more specific you are the better, even name a date you want to accomplish the affirmation. Write down the affirmation and read it out loud daily. In chapter seven you will have some more examples.

Subliminal (audio) messages are also masterful for helping self-esteem and other issues, and it works on a subconscious level which is where the majority of us operate from to do most of our daily tasks. You have driven home from work so many times, sometimes you don't even remember the drive, but you got there, even though your mind was busy running through the many things you still needed to tackle before going to bed.

Sexual Abuse

"Why did my family have to be rich which caused me to be left alone with a nanny for large chunks of time which gave her the opportunity to molest me?"

"Why did I have to be sent to boarding school where the girls held me down and "played doctor" on me like I am their baby doll?"

"Why did my mother have to be in denial which allowed her boyfriend to keep violating me?"

"Why did my mom have to be hooked on prescription medicine for migraines or depression that caused her to fall asleep which gave her girlfriend hours to force me to have oral sex with her. My mom never even heard my cries for help or saw my bruises."

"Why did my parents have to be in a cult that allowed the leader to sleep with all the females?"

"Why did God allow me to get date raped?"

"Why did God allow me to be gang raped?"

"How does this priest get away with brushing up against me or touching me while everyone prays?"

The definition of "Sexual Abuse" is any form of sexual violence including rape, groping, incest, molestation, and non-consensual sexual contact. 1 in 5 girls and 1 in 20 boys have been a victim of childhood sexual abuse. The most at risk are the children between the ages of 7-13 with 95% of these children being abused by someone they know.

Whether you were raped, molested, physically abused, bullied, emotionally abused, or someone was unfaithful to you and blamed you and then punished you for their own weakness, there is nothing you did or said or didn't say or didn't do that caused someone to harm you. The problem was theirs and will always be theirs. Abusers convince the person that if he or she tells, they will be rejected and be more alone and scared then they already are. Thinking that this silence is keeping the innocent one safe, is only protecting the evildoer. The thing that destroys "the abused" is the secrets eating away at their souls.

The abusers will always try to blame someone else. That is why I cling to the scriptures to help me stay grounded and connected to the truth. We have to move from regret and self-reproach to healing. What has shame, remorse, anger, self-loathing, punishment, depression done for any of us thus far? Has it erased even a second of our dreaded past? We cannot change the past. All we can do is learn and move forward.

There is a new therapy called **Emotional Freedom Technique** (**EFT**) also known as "tapping or psychological acupressure." EFT tapping has been used to treat people with anxiety and people with post-traumatic stress disorder (PTSD). It is good for those who are not ready to open up to a total stranger, even if that is their job to listen to us, due to bad experiences in the past or you just not wanting to risk exposing your child to someone who could damage them instead of helping them. My second counselor told me, "Many people get raped, get over it!" Then proceeded to teach me anatomy and healing colors. My college counselor did not want to talk about the rape either; she just wanted to talk about my mother. So, trust me, I understand about getting bad therapists. But if I would have given up, I would never have found a great counselor that helped me immensely. I would have never learned about these great new age treatments that work much faster.

"To those who have been called by God, **who LIVE in the LOVE of GOD the Father and the PROTECTION of Jesus Christ. May mercy, peace, and love be yours in full measure**." Jude 1:1.5-2 Good News Translation (GNT)

God is perfect. God gave everyone the freedom of "free will." Bad people use that "free will" to hurt other people. That does not make God flawed; it is the people who are using their power for evil that are flawed. We seem to forgot there is the devil at work also. If that makes you feel uncomfortable to use the word "devil" then use "dark forces" or "evil." There are Satan worshippers so there must be something they are worshipping. Some people practice witchcraft. Do you ever wonder who powers their spells? Certainly not God. Lucifer comes to steal your joy, your hope, your faith, your trust and your will to live and confuses you so that you blame God.

You need to believe in something good, something stronger than yourself; it helps you rely on someone other than yourself or be carried when life seems harsh. I know I have done much more than I ever thought I could because of my faith. I love myself because I learned from God and his people unconditional love.

Don't misunderstand me; I am aware that these so-called religious leaders or members have abused some of you. My molester was sitting next to me at a church at different times in my life. Then in another part of the country when I was still a teenager, the same church that helped open up my eyes to the scriptures that saved me from more years of molestation, eventually, changed leadership and that new minister was married with kids, and he molested or raped a teenager in the church and got her pregnant. I don't know what happened to that minister. God protected me before this was exposed. That sinister minister had asked me to travel to Africa on a mission team. After being in that church for seven years, I walked away never to return. This is what God has to say to these types of occurrences in the church:

"For some godless people have slipped in unnoticed among us, a person who distorts the message about the grace of our God in order **to excuse their immoral ways,** and who reject Jesus Christ, our only Master and Lord. Long ago the Scriptures predicted the condemnation they have received." Jude 1:4 Good News Translation (GNT)

Now, if you already knew that someone was coming to your home to steal your joy, safety and the very foundation of your life would you let him win? Would you step aside and give up? Lucifer will destroy you through those closest to you – your friends, family, neighbors, teachers, priests, police officers or even yourself.

Are you familiar with the saying, "I am my worst enemy?" We have the third drink or six drinks or the cake, cookies, ice cream way out of the portion of what is healthy for our bodies. We choose things that we know in advance are not good for us - the drugs or cigarettes or prescription pills when we aren't having symptoms. Each time we put it to our mouths we are announcing "I hate my life - take me out of this world." We do not realize yet how much more painful it is to die of liver failure, cancer, diabetes, heart attack or stroke. Or how slow and painful dying of high blood pressure, high cholesterol, and many other chronic illnesses will be.

Other times, we just run away by working ourselves to death, trying to prove we have value or we deserve to be here. Sometimes we over-work ourselves to stop our minds from thinking about the life we hate. We workout to change the bodies that we perceive as bad or dirty. No matter how many showers and baths we take, we feel dirty because of what some predator made us do. God feels your pain, your shame, your embarrassment, and your hopelessness. It is evident because he writes about it in his love note to us called the Bible.

"Jesus told this simple story, but they had no idea what he was talking about. So, he tried again. "I'll be explicit, then. I am the Gate for the sheep. **All those others are up to no good** - sheep stealers, every one of them. But the sheep didn't listen to them. I am the Gate. **Anyone who goes through me will be cared for** - will freely go in and out and find pasture. **A thief is only there to steal and kill and destroy. I came so they can have** real and eternal life, **more and better life than they ever dreamed of.**" John 10:10 The Message (MSG)

"In a few minutes, **you're going to do battle with your enemies.** Don't waiver in resolve. **Don't fear.** Don't hesitate. **Don't panic.** GOD, **your God, is right there with you, fighting with you against your enemies, fighting to win.**" Deuteronomy 20:3-4

The serious long-term consequences of sexual child abuse are discussed below. One-third of abused children will eventually victimize their children. 80% of abused children will meet the criteria for at least one psychiatric disorder at age 21 (including but not limited to anxiety, depression, post-traumatic stress disorder, and eating disorders). Abused children are 25% more likely to experience teen pregnancy. Sexually abused teens are three times less likely to practice safe sex. 14.4% of all men imprisoned in the United States were abused as children. 36.7% of all women in prison were abused as children. Children who have been sexually abused are 2.5 times more likely to develop alcohol abuse. Children who have been sexually abused are 3.8 times more likely to develop drug addictions. EMDR (Eye Movement Desensitization Reprocessing) would help to change this trend.

I discovered that when you have past hurts you see things through that hurt like a dirty window. People who are trying to help you could look like the bad guys. The people who care about you the most can hurt you because they tell you the truth. The truth is not easy to hear, but it is necessary for change. This is where we have to take responsibility for our choices and forgive the bad decisions we made when we were in despair.

In my life, I have surmised abused people are very hard people; it is their form of self-protection. They can act like they don't care, but they genuinely do. They tend to habitually not want to talk about what hurts them because this picks at the pain that they have shoved down and locked away. They manage to avoid sad movies, scary nonfiction books, and the news to evade tapping into that sadness or pain. They might shun scary movies because they feel scared all the time.

The abused may not like to cry or for you to cry. They will make you feel uncomfortable or weak for crying or make you feel wrong for showing emotions other than joy. They could even be distrusting of your happiness. The walking wounded usually have a tiny range of emotions. Anger is the dominant feeling which usually is covering up sadness. They also experience momentary joy based on a short-lived circumstance. They may be very quiet, or they can be the kind of person who is always cracking jokes and never wants to be serious. What I have seen is fear runs most of the decisions they make.

"There is no fear in love. But perfect love drives out fear because fear has to do with punishment. The one who fears is not made perfect in love." 1 John 4:18 New International Version (NIV)

A wise spiritual teacher once said, "Learning new things is not the difficult part, but rather letting go of the old things, those old stories of who we were, how we use to do things, and what everyone feels comfortable with and thinks we ought to be. In short, we cannot change until we move on and move forward until we get emotionally unstuck from yesterday's thinking and living. Only then can we pursue God's dream of who we are meant to be."

"So, what do you think? **With God on our side like this, how can we lose?** If God didn't hesitate to put everything on the line for us, embracing our condition and exposing himself to the worst by sending his own Son, is there anything else he wouldn't gladly and freely do for us? And **who would dare tangle with God by messing with one of God's chosen**? Who would dare even to point a finger? The One who died for us - who was raised to life for us! - Is in the presence of God at this very moment **sticking up for us. Do you think anyone is going to be able to drive a wedge between us and Christ's love for us? There**

is no way! Not trouble, not hard times, not hatred, not hunger, not homelessness, **not bullying** threats, **not backstabbing**, not even the worst sins listed in Scriptures... I'm absolutely convinced that nothing - nothing living or dead, angelic or demonic, today or tomorrow, high or low, thinkable or unthinkable - **absolutely *nothing* can get between us and God's love because of the way that Jesus our Master has embraced us.**" Romans 8:31-39 The Message (MSG)

This is why Satan comes after us when we are children when we are optimistic, loving and forgiving because if we kept developing that character; we would be a force for good. When we enter college, we again get back that feeling of we can change the world! The college years is the age that most rapes and domestic violence occur. These are all schemes of the evil one's plots to destroy hope, power, faith, and plant fear, and blaming mostly against God, others and oneself.

If we actually knew who our Creator really is and who he is not, we would be unstoppable! We could achieve anything with our faith. If we could forgive and love others deeply; this world would be a different place. We would respect each other and work together to achieve things far beyond what our minds can image at this primitive stage in our life. We would not have churches with all one nationality in them.

Our Creator is the maker of all nationalities because there is not one kind of monkey or cat or wolf or bear because they come in all colors, shapes, and sizes. We would not have different religions fighting with each other. We would learn to accept people where they are at and not pass judgment on them. We would love those people who are different and like them because they are unique and bond with them over how we are the same. We cry, love, laugh, hunger, thirst, bleed and need and dream just like everyone else. Be impressed with them that they can speak more than one language and that they value the culture of their ancestors. We would not fight so hard to make everyone just like us.

When you visit a church, and you see 3 to 5 or more different races, languages being spoken, the lesson being translated into other dialects these are signs that God is there.

Jehovah is not this punishing, angry, old man full of rules that looks at women as second-rate citizens. Not the God that we created by putting the image of our parents on the creator we call Father. Not the God that people used to control you and keep you from doing anything that they couldn't relate to or feared. Not the kind of God that condones a person being considered property. Not the God that humans slapped all their human-made rules under his title and said it is from God. Not the God that states money is evil. If money was evil why are the people who were God's favorite the richest men in the world or that country (Abraham, Job, Moses (the son of a Princess), Joseph, David, Solomon, etc.)? It is greed, envy, jealousy, pride, anger, selfishness, prejudice, violence, liars, thieves, murders, perversion, and obsession for power that destroys families, marriages, and society.

There are plenty of wealthy and influential people in the world that do great things to help the less fortunate, but there are also prosperous and powerful people who do terrible things. It is not the money that makes them dangerous; it is how they use the money. They would be deplorable people with or without currency. The good rich would still be good with or without money. The Pharisees had no wealth or possession, yet their jealousy and fear of losing their prestige made them kill an innocent man who was healing people and feeding the homeless who happened to be the Son of God.

Eventually, what is hidden always gets exposed. The predators usually convince their innocent ones that their actions are the norm or if they tell their parents or friends, they will get mad at them. They always weave some lie that is believed, but hopefully not forever. That is why it is so important to do the work of healing because otherwise, you may hold onto these lies until they destroy you.

You are not at fault or to blame. You are not bad, nor do you make others do bad things to you. What you wear cannot make a moral person turn bad. It may cause them lust, but it does not make them tear your clothes off, hit you, strangle you and do whatever they want to your body without your permission. It does not make a person crawl into your bed when you are sleeping and touch you in your private places. It does not give any person the right to bump you and rub their body against you or kiss you without your permission. Just because they are older than you, stronger than you, or in a position of power does not give them the authority to violate your boundaries. What belongs to you is your personal space and your body.

"Those people will cheer at the spectacle, shouting 'Good riddance!' and calling for a celebration, **for these two prophets pricked the conscience of all the people on earth, made it impossible for them to enjoy their sins.**" Revelation 11:7 The Message (MSG)

Freedom of speech does not permit a person to say things to you that make you feel uncomfortable. Nor is it legal for them to show you pictures or DVDs of body parts or sexual activity to try to get you aroused so they can take advantage of you. No one should be able to excuse away slapping you on the buttocks or grabbing your breast no matter if they are the President of the USA or the King/Queen of another country or the Pope or your boss.

"**The good times of the wicked are short-lived; godless joy is only momentary.** The evil might become world famous, strutting at the head of the celebrity parade, but still, end up in a pile of dung." Job 20:5-6 The Message (MSG)

Rapist and molesters are rarely cured, repentant or changed. They will still be molesting anyone even as a senior citizen. Molesters will rape babies, and the elderly, so it has nothing to do with sex appeal or what you wear or what you say or do or how you look. Do not believe this lie that if you are raped, it was lust, or if it was by someone you were dating or married to that it was an act of passion or kinky sex. **The truth is that it was a display of power, control, and dominance. It is violence to the utmost degree.**

If you get into a fight at school by a bully, you can heal from the outer wounds that were caused by getting beat up, but rape affects your soul. Intimacy was created to bind a couple for life; they become one flesh. If you are violated sexually, it changes every relationship you are intimate with until you heal. There could be 10-20 memories that are affecting you that happened at any timeframe in your life. If someone you know wears the same cologne as your predator, it will trigger negative memories. If someone laughs like them, it may upset your whole day. You might ask, "Why would someone laugh while forcing you to have sex with them?" For the fact that they are sick and insane, they will laugh because you cry. When you are sexually violated, it even affects your pregnancy, your ability to have that child be affectionate to you and feel comfortable with it. Things that are supposed to be a joy and the happiest moments of your life will be tainted because of this sexual assault against your body. It is so vital to complete your healing process.

CHAPTER FIVE

JUST THE FACTS

"First of all, you must understand that in the last days **some people will appear whose lives are controlled by their own lusts.**" 2 Peter 3:3 Good News Translation (GNT)

"The LORD detests the thoughts of the wicked." Proverbs 15:26 New International Version (NIV)

Why? Because thoughts become actions and their actions will hurt others.

Below are some statistics of on assault and rape. The population is listed so you will have an idea of the gravity of these particular crimes. These facts come from the Countries-with-the-Highest-and-Lowest-Crime-Rates. The Crime rate is calculated as follows: Result of <u>Number of Crimes</u> divided by Population is multiplied by 100,000 based on the Almanac 1998-2018.

1. California 39,540,000
    Los Angeles 4 mill
    (58.5 rapes & 396.1 assaults per 100,000)
    (2,343 rapes reported & 15,874 assaults in 2016)

    San Francisco 880K
    (39.3 rapes & 300.3 assaults per 100,000)
    (342 rapes reported & 2,616 assaults)

2. Texas 28,305,000
    Houston 2.3 mill
    (51.8 rapes & 534.9 assaults per 100,000)
    (1,210 rapes reported & 12,487 assaults)

San Antonio 1.5 mil
(79.4 rapes & 479.3 assaults per 100,000)
(1,190 rapes reported & 7,183 assaults)

3. Florida 21,000,000
   Jacksonville 880K
   (58.7 rapes & 388.2 assaults per 100,000)
   (517 rapes reported & 3,418 assaults)

   Miami 450K
   (20 rapes & 534.2 assaults per 100,000)
   (90 rapes reported & 2,401 assaults)

4. New York 19,850,000
   New York 8.5 mill
   (27.7 rapes & 360.4 assaults per 100,000)
   (2372 rapes reported & 30,873 assaults)

5. Pennsylvania 13,000,000
   Philadelphia 1.6 mill
   (80.1 rapes & 496.7 assaults per 100,000)
   (1,259 rapes reported & 7,803 assaults)

6. Illinois 13,000,000
   Chicago 2.7 mill
   (58.3 rapes & 580.3 assaults per 100,000)
   (1,589 rapes reported & 15,815 assaults)

7. Ohio 12,000,000
   Cleveland 390K
   (126.4 rapes & 698.0 assaults per 100,000)
   (488 rapes reported & 2,696 assaults)

Jennifer Gamboa

8. Georgia 10,430,000
   Atlanta 470K
   (28.8 rapes & 593.3 assaults per 100,000)
   (136 rapes reported & 2,804 assaults)

9. Michigan 10,000,000
   Detroit 680K
   (86.5 rapes & 1,475.6 assaults per 100,000)
   (579 rapes reported & 9,882 assaults)

"I hate my life, so I will complain without holding
back; I will speak because I am so unhappy. John
10:1 New Century Version (NCV)

When you are violated you begin to hate your
existence.

1. China 1,415,000,000
   (Rapes 32,000 per year in China)
   (Rapes 26.8 per million in 2011 Singapore)
   (Assaults 14.6 in 2011 in Singapore)

2. India 1,355,500,000
   (Rapes 22,172 per 100,000 in India in 2010)
   (Rapes 18.39 per million in India)
   (Assaults 23.1 per 100,000 in 2011)

3. Indonesia 268,000,000
   (14,599 assaults occurred in 2015 in Indonesia)

4. Brazil 212,000,000
   (Rapes in Brazil 12.3 per 100,000 in 2012)
   (Assaults 17,800 per 100,000)

96

5. Russia 149,000,000
   (Rapes 4,907 per 100,000 in 2015)
   (34.46 rapes per million in 2015 in Russia)
   "Russia is one of three countries in Europe
   and Central Asia that have not enacted laws
   specifically targeting domestic violence says the
   Library of Congress."

6. Mexico 131,000,000
   Data includes all 32 states in Mexico
   (Rape 14,993 per 100,000 in 2015)
   (127.18 Rapes per million in 2015)
   (223.5 assaults per 100,000)
   (45,452 assaults in 2015 in Mexico)

7. Japan 127,000,000
   (51 assaults per 100,000 in 2011 in Japan)
   (1289 rapes per 100,000 in 2010 in Japan)
   (10.11 rapes per million in Japan in 2010)

8. Philippines 107,000,000
   (Rapes 5,813 per 100,000 in Philippines 2015)
   (63.26 Rapes per million in 2015 in the
   Philippines)

   All statistics on assaults and rapes are from
Nation Master.

   "Each heart knows its own bitterness, and
no one else can share its joy." Proverbs 14:10 New
International Version (NIV)

"God's anger is revealed from heaven against all the sin and evil of the people whose evil ways prevent the truth from being known." Romans 1:18 Good News Translation (GNT)

I expose this so that people will not sweep it under the rug or downplay it any longer. Laws must be changed to protect the human race. We can no longer accept inequality by gender or race or religion. These are crimes that affect all of us, the young or the elderly, male or female, gay or heterosexual. We have to start protecting the innocent people in this country instead of the corrupt. We have to stop filling our prisons with small crimes and start filling them up with the violations that destroy people's whole being. When we do nothing to solve or prevent the problems or heal the results of the issues, we are a part of the problem. If you turn a blind eye, you are promoting a corrupt world instead of trying to make it better for everyone. Unscrupulous people do evil things; there is no gray area here.

"You know that such people are corrupt, and their sins prove that they are wrong." Titus 3:11 Good News Translation (GNT)

Does your life matter to you? Does your life matter to at least one person? If your answer is no, I guarantee you are wrong about how much people care about you! It is natural to be afraid of a familiar situation that reminds you of a bad experience; this is what is called Post Traumatic Stress Disorder. Men and women who have fought in a war experience

PTSD. But let's talk about what many people don't know. 14,900 military members experienced unwanted sexual contact, 43% were females, and 17% were males reported by the Department of Defense, Fiscal Year 2016 Annual Report on Sexual Assault in the Military dated 2017. Sexual assault in the military often goes unreported. We all deserve to be protected. When the ones protecting us are not safe; there is a real problem. An estimated 80,600 inmates each year experience sexual violence while in prison or jail. 60% of all sexual violence against inmates is perpetrated by jail or prison staff. More than 50% of the sexual contact between inmate and staff member, all of which is illegal, is nonconsensual based on the Department of Justice, Office of Justice Programs, Bureau of Justice Statistics, Sexual Victimization in Prisons and Jails Reported by Inmates, 2011-2012 dated 2013. We all matter! We have a right to be safe even when serving time for a crime.

American Indians are twice as likely to experience a rape/sexual assault compared to all races. On average, American Indians ages 12 and older experience 5,900 sexual assaults per year according to the Department of Justice, Office of Justice Programs, Bureau of Justice Statistics, American Indians and Crime, 1992-2002 dated 2004.

"200,000 Caucasians are sexually assaulted on average annually. 57% of the predators are white people. 49,000 Hispanics are sexually assaulted, and an estimated 25,000 African Americans are sexually assaulted annually. 27% of the predators are African American according to RAINN.

The average number of rapes and sexual assaults against females of childbearing age is approximately 250,000 in a year. Thus, the number of children conceived from rape each year in the United States might range from 7,750 - 12,500. Studies suggest that the chance of getting pregnant from one-time, unprotected intercourse is between 3.1-5%, depending on the time of month intercourse occurs, whether contraceptives are used, and the age of the female.

"People who have been sexually assaulted are more likely to use drugs than the general public, 3.4 times more likely to use marijuana, six times more likely to use cocaine, and ten times more likely to use other major drugs," according to RAINN.

"The likelihood that a person suffers suicidal or depressive thoughts increases after sexual violence. 94% of women who are raped experience post-traumatic stress disorder (PTSD) symptoms during the two weeks following the rape based on a Journal of Traumatic Stress dated 1992. 30% of women report PTSD symptoms nine months after the rape based on Post Traumatic Stress Disorder: DSM-IV and Beyond, American Psychiatric Press. 33% of women who are raped contemplate suicide. 13% of women who are raped attempt suicide, based on Rape in America: A Report to the Nation. Arlington, VA: dated 1992. Approximately 70% of raped or sexually assaulted people experience moderate to severe distress, a larger percentage than for any other violent crime," based on Department of Justice, Socio-emotional Impact of Violent Crime dated 2014.

Every year in the USA 60,000 children are sexually assaulted according to RAINN investigation called "How Often Does Sexual Assault Occur in the United States?" How is America going to stay a world leader with these crimes destroying our youth and our college students before they even get a chance to do great things? We will have more people in prison or mental hospitals or dead than we have to make our society better. Something needs to be done now!

"GOD examines every heart and sees through every motive." 1 Chronicle 28:9.5 The Message (MSG)

CHAPTER SIX

HEALING

Keep in mind, even as fast as specific treatments work if you have many traumas you may need to deal with the major ones first. A person may discover that some of their chronic physical pain is linked to a childhood trauma that they do not even remember. I have found this scenario applies to a few people. If a person is going through a lot in their life, it might be better for them to go through the smaller issues first, so that they won't get overwhelmed. We love big things, big trips, big cars, etc. but remember it is the little things in life that make up our lives. It is the small things or the repetitive things that could be causing trouble in a person's life. There is no "you have to" or "you should" when it comes to treatment except you must to be willing and not give up. When I say this, understand I do not mean if you have a therapist who is not right for you, stay with them anyway. I mean make sure you are not quitting because it gets uncomfortable.

You can choose a different method of treatment or a new therapist but don't stop treatment until significant progress is accomplished. I know emergencies come up that have to be addressed, but don't let that keep you away from therapy for too long. Sometimes when you are going through challenging life circumstances, it is better to be in treatment, so you handle them victoriously. Remember the saying, "That's the straw that broke the camel's back" which means to me when a person's life is overwhelming, it only takes one more thing to push that person over the edge. We all have our limits on what we can handle. As we face the past, this is the time to be brave, and it will encourage you when you discover how strong you are. This time of healing is the perfect time to learn to lean on someone else; don't carry the load alone any longer.

"Here are proverbs **that will help you recognize wisdom and good advice and understand sayings with deep meaning. They can teach you how to live intelligently** and how to be honest, just and fair. They can make an inexperienced person clever and **teach young people how to be resourceful."** Proverbs 1:2-4 Good News Translation (GNT)

I know that some people can get scared away by religion due to bad experiences or misunderstandings. Consider, "righteousness" as "making an effort to do the right thing." Many famous people quote scriptures but leave out that it is from the Bible and people soak it up. But I want you to be aware of where the wisdom originated.

"God, I invite your searching gaze into my heart. Examine me through and through; **find out everything that may be hidden within me.** Put me to the test and **sift through all my anxious cares. See if there is any path of pain I'm walking on,** and **lead me back to your glorious, everlasting ways** - the path that brings me back to you." Psalm 139:23-24 The Passion Translation (TPT)

"Now, the "Lord" I'm referring to is the Holy Spirit, and **wherever he is Lord, there is freedom."** 2 Corinthians 3:17 The Passion Translation (TPT)

The issue with the religious is that they carry a Bible but don't read it or they have had the same Bible for years and never read it from cover to cover. The most significant error is when they read the Bible, they don't apply it to their lives thus making it empty and useless. There is a church on every other street corner. If we all practiced love your neighbor, wouldn't our neighborhoods be very different then they are now? If we put into action, "Do to others as you would like them to do to you," crime would almost be erased. If we valued the scripture below, we would no longer have domestic violence. That is what 2 Corinthians 3:17 means - Jesus or God should be Lord of your marriage, your job, your finances, when you drive on the road, and when you deal with people (meaning Lord of your emotions).

"Husbands, in the same way, be considerate as you live with your wives, and treat them with respect as the weaker partner and as heirs with you of the gracious gift of life, **so that nothing will hinder your prayers."** 1 Peter 3:7 New International Version (NIV)

Then people would not have a distaste for religion. I don't care if you read the Quran if it was obeyed and followed. There would not be violence, killing, and wars. **Quran 76:8 "And they give food in spite of love for it, to the needy, the orphan, and the captive."** It is love that the world has deducted which makes this world so full of pain. In different states and different regions, we call the male that gave his sperm to create us by different names – father, dad, daddy, dada, pop, poppa, pa, sir, etc. why is it not ok for people from different regions to call their Creator by a name that means something to them and their culture? I am not condoning cults. My purpose is to show if that belief makes a person better and their society then why be against? In the Bible, God and Jesus are called by many names. We need to be more open-minded. We need to stop finding issues with the slightest differences. We were all created in God's image.

There are a lot of areas Americans can do things better, but do you see Canada or France waging war with the USA because we don't provide more for our citizens in the way of healthy lunches in school, free college and help for the poor? We have to stop thinking we are so much better than everyone else.

"It's easy to see a smudge on your neighbor's face and be oblivious to the ugly sneer on your own. Do you have the nerve to say, **'Let me wash your face for you,' when your own face is distorted by contempt?** It's this I-know-better-than-you-mentality again, **playing a holier-than-thou part instead of just living your own part. Wipe that ugly sneer off your own face,** and you might be fit to offer a washcloth to your neighbor." Luke 6:41-42 The Message (MSG)

This lack of self-examination is how many people think, that have not been violated. If you have been abused, usually you look at yourself with contempt. You might not even be able to look at yourself in the mirror. You only see what's wrong with you most of the time. Webster's dictionary says "acceptance is admittance to or approval to or to receive willingly." Does that sound like you? Do you willingly receive a gift from someone other than on Christmas or your birthday? Or do you say, "You shouldn't have" or "You did not have to?" Do you accept compliments? When someone says, "That is a nice dress," or "Your hair looks nice," do you do a redirect – with comments like this "This old thing," or "I have a good hairdresser." If you had bad hair, there is nothing a hairdresser could do to make it look nice.

If you were not shaped decently, everything on you would not look right. So, what, you have a few extra pounds on you! Does that mean you can never look good? Does that mean that a color cannot bring out your eyes or your perfect skin tone? Is being overweight so devastating that a dress or shorts cannot show off your beautiful shapely legs? We caring weight in different places that doesn't mean there is nothing good about our bodies.

If you have one pimple, you say, "I look terrible." Does that one pimple take away your dimples, or your bright shining eyes or your pretty white teeth or your scar-free face or your long thick, shiny hair or your curled eyelashes? No. Those who have low self-esteem tend to overlook the 80-90% of the good they have going on and focus way too much on the 10-20% that needs improvement. Notice, I didn't say failure, a disaster beyond redemption, or a total mess. People get surgery to improve their looks, but no matter what they have reconstructed; they see something wrong because it is not what is on the outside that is the issue, the problem is in the inside -our thoughts and opinions that someone taught us are wrong. These beliefs cause us to be eccentric.

"And **even the very hairs of your head are all numbered**." Matthew 10:30 New International Version (NIV)

God knows every detail about you including how many hairs you have on your head. There is something unique about you. Why don't you spend some time just learning about you? Webster's dictionary says, "Trust is reliance on the character, ability, strength, or truth of someone or something and dependence on some future hope." What are your strengths? What unique ability do you have that will give the world a brighter future?

If you don't take the time to figure out what you want, you will be striving after someone else's dream but thinking it is your own. You won't discover you have been chasing the wrong dream all your life until you are on your death bed - full of regret. I have buried more of my family than most people my age. I know about their secrets and their regrets that come out even after they are dead.

Trust in you. But you have to know who you are. What do you want? What is your deepest desire? What do you value? What secret hope do you have that you have been afraid to share or speak out loud? Did you use to win awards or trophies in school or sports? When it stopped that is probably the time period something major changed in your life. If you figure out what it was and work through it, your life will start succeeding again. Trust is also choosing to give someone a chance. I think you should decide to give yourself a chance. You have been patiently waiting for your turn. You have sacrificed so much to so many others; when is it is your turn?

Or you could have given to no one, and hidden in your room, your house, your work for fear of being hurt again. Isn't it about time you lived? Your goal of never being hurt again has taken away your opportunities to have fun, to laugh, to trust, to love deeply, and to have the wonder of a child about the littlest things!

Our wound is not on the outside, but we have to work just as hard to recover! You have seen in the movies when someone gets into a car accident and has to have many surgeries and go through much physical therapy to get back to being able to do the basics in life that they use to take for granted. We who have been abused have mental and emotional challenges. We have to do more than survive the day; we can choose to THRIVE!

We can accept our role to motivate, to inspire change in thinking, and bring others with us into peace, joy and a fantastic life, whatever that looks like for you! Once you start this journey what you think is possible will change. You will feel and want things you never even thought about before. You will be another person, the person who has been waiting to come out all your life! You will find your purpose for why you are here. You will be the best part of you. You have to believe you can have more than the current limits you have set for your life!

What is a big part of the healing process? It is accepting our part of the responsibility. It is essential to keep this in mind; as long as we stay stuck in hatred, anger, bitterness, lack of forgiveness and insecurity which is another form of fear, we live the first part of this scripture. We can take hold of the second half of the scripture and make it our life.

"Hope deferred makes the heart sick, but **a longing fulfilled is a tree of life**." Proverbs 13:12 New International Version (NIV)

Do not misunderstand what I mean by forgiveness. Forgiveness is not saying what anyone did to us to hurt us was ok, forgotten, acceptable, did not affect us, or had a minimal effect. It is the door to letting go of the hold the offender has on us that keeps us stuck. What they did will never be condoned.

By this act of forgiveness, we are saying, "I am releasing the hold you have on me and not letting it interrupt my happiness, joy, my ability to love and be loved, and my ability to trust." I forgive myself because what happened to me was not my fault. I did not allow anyone to do anything to me. It was a case of innocence, ignorance, not enough physical strength or weak boundaries, or a matter of being in the wrong place at the wrong time or lack of seeing someone's real character. We all get fooled by the wolf in sheep's clothing sooner or later. I do not suggest you write or talk to the person who hurt you; this is an exercise to alleviate your heart.

Do not live in denial or else when it happens to your child or your relative and they come to you, your natural response will be to deny. Now you have just turned into the people who hurt you as a child. Be an advocate for yourself; trust your memories, your

111

feelings and the person who gives you proof that it occurred.

I thought what I was remembering was a dream. One day, I shared it with two different relatives and they both verified, yes, it happened. They caught the person in the act. If you want to be able to trust yourself, you must start being honest with yourself. You must begin to love yourself enough to tear down the wall of denial that keeps you from healing.

Do you trust a liar? If someone was lying to you every day, would you want to be around them? No, you want to have healthy friendships and love relationships. It starts with you becoming the person you would want to attract into your life. You can start by facing the truth about your past. Do you want to keep hanging around that family member that abused you; only to make everyone else in the family feel comfortable or to prevent exposing the horrible truth? You don't have to tell a verbal lie; you can just be living a lie.

As an unhealed person, we can admire the traits we do not possess. If we are timid, or lack confidence, or don't speak up for ourselves or don't like making decisions instead of overcoming these weaknesses in ourselves, we find a mate that is outspoken, talkative or bold in their comments. We feel like that person balances us out. As time passes, we discover that the person is controlling, insecure, jealous, violent and tears down the little confidence we have. Two half people don't make a whole person. Two whole and complete people with high to medium self-esteem make a healthy relationship. You don't want to go into a relationship needy or desperate; it is a recipe for disaster. You have to be comfortable with yourself and happy being single. There is a difference from being alone and being lonely. You need to be at ease with silence and being by yourself. It is normal to need others, but there is a big difference in being needy.

"Keep vigilant watch over **your heart; that's where life starts**." Proverbs 4:23 The Message (MSG)

"Above all else, **guard your heart**, for everything you do flows from it." Proverbs 4:23 The New International Version (NIV)

This scripture does not mean put your heart on a shelf, as Grandma did with the good china, waiting for a special occasion that never came. What you don't use you lose one way or another.

Test out that heart; see how many people it can love. I bet you it will never get too full. It will fill up but with joy, compassion, gratitude, peace, and love for yourself and others. You must learn to love yourself to love others effectively. It is your choice. What will you choose? If your heart stays broken, it won't love properly. Choose Healing. Choose Bravery, Calm, Positive Feelings, and Life. Choose Love. You deserve to be happy! Your journey to happiness started when you picked up this book.

The memories of the abuse get lodged in your cells, muscles, and tissues even if your mind does not choose to recall it. It can show up as back pain that is there more than it is gone. Our body is always sending us messages because it wants us to be in the best physical, emotional/mental and spiritual health. I

113

know you may be surprised I said spiritual, but there is a spirit that lives within us, and that requires nurturing, or we will feel hallow.

Now, let's finish discussing the physical messages from the body. When your back hurts, it could be your body saying that you don't feel supported in the current situation. When you start getting the support you need by others, or you are doing self-care, you will find that the back pain will go away or be less frequent.

It is possible that you have a physical issue that needs to be taken care of, as well, which your body also wants you to resolve. I am speaking to those of you who hate to go to the doctor. You break your finger, and you let it grow all mangled and twisted rather than go to the doctor and get a splint to help it heal and be properly functional again. Unprocessed memories can show itself as anxiety or tight shoulders. It can show up as an uneasy feeling when you return to the house where the abuse took place.

"For **whatever is hidden is meant to be disclosed, and whatever is concealed is meant to be brought out into the open**." Mark 4:22 New International Version (NIV)

By abusing you, the predator tried to cover your light. Eventually, the truth starts to poke holes in the bag that you were stuffed in, which allows the light to come in and warm you, give you life, and bring back the joy that was stolen from you. Have you ever watched a baby or a child? A child finds so much pleasure in every little thing that he or she explores. When you hear them laugh, it makes you smile or chuckle. They are care-free and empowered. When a human is beaten or molested or emotionally abused or kidnapped as a child, that light is replaced with fear. Healing will get back that rare joy and trust.

It will enable you to enjoy life. Don't be surprised if you want to do some things that you wanted to do as a child or loved as a child. It is ok. You are free! Nurture your inner child. Eventually, you will move through different stages of your life; and it will no longer matter that you got stuck at a certain age due to trauma.

When I started my healing, I started vacationing to all kinds of different amusement parks. Then one day, I no longer needed to do that. I use to begin tasks and never finish them even if it would only take a few more minutes to complete. Now I am doing huge undertakings and finishing them all. I remodeled my cabinets and countertops with my own hands. As I made over the inside of my mind and heart, I transformed my living environment to reflect the new me. My hobbies changed, my unhealthy friendships were replaced, and my relationships deepened.

"Jesus went on: "Does anyone bring a lamp home and put it under a washtub or beneath the bed? Don't you put it up on a table or on the mantel? **We're not keeping secrets, we're telling them; we're not hiding things, we're bringing them out into the open."** Mark 4:21-22 The Message (MSG)

You cannot continue to live with this secret and think you will thrive; some action will help, even if you have to write down the details of your abuse in a journal because it would be too uncomfortable to speak it aloud. This method will provide you some freedom. You might have to write down what happened to you in bits and pieces. Remove the pain from your body and put it on paper. Release yourself from the hold it has had on you for years. I am talking about writing down what that person said that hurt you. Write down how it made you feel. Journal what you wish you would have said or done. If this causes you anger or sadness, punch a pillow or scream into a pillow. If you are not home alone, go somewhere you can be alone to write, cry, scream and get it out. It has been trapped for years needing to be released. You can rip up the pages after if it will make you feel better.

Don't think that one-time journal entry will fix all your problems. You will deal with the big stuff and then eventually the only things left will be the little stuff and those things matter also. Don't stop until you reach the finish line. Get it all out; why hold onto it any longer? Replace it with the good and the positive, because that space needs to be filled up so that the pain cannot return.

I wrote in my journal about the little stuff every day on my way to work on the commuter train. It changed my relationships in my family and my friendships. I eventually was able to talk to many of the people that I had these feelings about and hear their side. It was a major healing event. I am not talking about the predators. I am talking about the good people that were not there for me in the way that I hoped for in the past. I wished they could be closer. I never spoke up about what I wanted or asked for what I needed from others due to the abuse; my response to being abused made me feel more unloved and under-valued. I did not ask because I did not think I mattered. Once I did start speaking up about what I wanted, I started getting what I declared. My family was hardly ever around because we lived so far away from each other. They started calling more often, texting and inviting me to family reunions, etc. All I wanted was to be a part of a good family. They became everything I had hoped for in a family as a child but I experienced as an adult but it healed my inner child's longing. The other side of my family that I spent more of my time with as a child did not talk much about feelings, but when I started asking more questions, I found out our real history. It made me understand them better and to able to let go of the blame game. We cannot demonstrate that in which we have no experience. Broken homes become like a cookie cutter factory, you could add frosting or sprinkles but underneath the cookies are the same. Only through healing from your past can you break out of the cookie factory.

"As water reflects the face, so **one's life reflects the heart**." Proverbs 27:19 New International Version (NIV)

The shame of what happened to the person keeps the beauty inside of them from being fully realized by the individual and others. Those who have been abused somehow believe that there is something wrong with them, and that they did something wrong. The mind has to make sense of it, so it comes to these false conclusions that are not helpful. These unprocessed memories assumption is the furthest thought from the truth. Only the predator did something wrong and the people who blamed you or did not believe you, or sided with the offender or ignored you; they are wrong and unhealthy for you.

"Knowing what is right is like deep water in the heart; a wise person draws from the well within." Proverbs 20:5 The Message (MSG)

The scripture above emphasizes the need for healthy people in your life to help you uncover what is buried deep inside you. It also shows that if you stay on the surface or shallow waters you will not discover the truth that is in your heart. Journaling helps to get beneath the surface when others are not available. Journaling after counseling sessions are very beneficial as well. Until you expose the truth to the light, you will not see the truth about yourself and others. This false truth keeps you from discovering how to evaluate things and know if how others said you should see things is the correct viewpoint. Have you ever had a thought and you believed it until you questioned it or heard yourself say it out loud? Then you reflect on it and say that is not true at all.

It is just like the nursery rhymes we are taught to quote in elementary school in the USA, "Roses are red and violets are blue," but in reality, violets are lavender or purple. There are indoor versions, wild or outdoor versions, flowers and plants which would be other combinations of colors. Let us examine the rest of the nursery rhyme. Some roses are red, but they do come in many other colors. We are familiar with seeing red roses because it symbolizes love. Each color of a rose symbolizes a different meaning. When we believe in this black and white way of thinking, we reduce all the different possibilities in life.

Let us look at another example of overgeneralizing. If your father or your husband beat you, you could conclude that all men are evil. Especially, if there are not very many males in your family or your husband was your first boyfriend. If you are a male, then you will start thinking you are flawed. But you have coworkers, neighbors, and friends that are males. Is every one of them bad? No.

You are not bad either. You might have made a mistake and broken something, but you are not bad. One act of wrongdoing does not make someone wicked. Without realizing it, parents can label a child as bad instead of the action as wrong and this becomes the child's belief system that effects the direction of their life. We make many mistakes in life that is how we learn. This need to label everyone is ignorance because it has long-term effects. For example, we might have been called, "lazy," now we never think it is alright to relax and do nothing on the weekends. Even the Creator allowed himself 24 hours of rest after inventing the universe in six days. The previous statement should give us all the permission we need to take a vacation, a break or sit on the couch and do nothing because we aren't everlasting, so we need a lot more breaks than just a day.

By the seventh day God had finished his work. **On the seventh day he rested from all his work. God blessed the seventh day. He made it a Holy Day because on that day he rested from his work, all the creating God had done.** Genesis 2:2-3 New International Version (NIV)

"Do not accuse anyone for no reason - when they have done you no harm." Proverbs 3:30 New International Version (NIV)

The scripture above makes me think of all the fortune-telling that people did that was false, but we believed them and made it real. Like people telling you, "You will be fat one day; it is in our family genes." So then for years, you stress over getting fat. Or you give up trying to be healthy and eat whatever you want because why restrict yourself if you are going to be fat anyway? Or they call you lazy, but you are not, they are accusing you falsely. Or you are a jealous and insecure person, so you blame your boyfriend, girlfriend or spouse of flirting or cheating on you, but they are not even thinking about it. After a while, they feel like if I am going to be punished for it, I might as well commit the act. Your words have just created your worst nightmare, an unfaithful partner or an end to that relationship.

Try this and see if it does not become real for you. When you believe God loves to bless you. You will see blessings happening to you more frequently.

"His master **recognized that GOD was with him**, saw that **GOD was working for good in everything he did**." Genesis 39:3 The Message (MSG)

Life was not meant to be like some zombie movie where you walk around from place to place only feeling your hunger, but ignoring that you are half dead or obviously wounded and falling apart. All your emotions are turned off expect the basic instinct to feed. Zombies drag themselves pitifully around and then attack! Then they pull themselves away, acting like nothing gruesome and awful just happened. They repeat this course of action again and again never satisfied, never healing or bonding with anyone even though now half the population are zombies.

You may think this is silly to compare the big screen to real life but don't you go through life in a crowd of people not interacting on a deep level. When you are at work, or a family reunion how many of those people, actually know who you are? How many of those Facebook friends are there for you when you are going through tough times?

Parents, think back on how many deep-talks you have had with your teenager or your friends that was not interrupted by a phone call or a text. A video, a movie, a TV show or music or electronic games or the phone has more time with the younger culture than they have an in-depth, meaningful exchange with another human being. We would be shocked if we knew what these kids were exposed to daily at school or social media. There is so much more violence at school than we realize. There are so many more villains advertising to our children than you realize; exposing them to things that steal their innocence. Start substituting some of that electronic device time to devote to your healing. You will find that your quality of life increases, your anxiety decreases and your happiness goes to higher levels than you have ever known. You might ascertain that you don't want to spend so much time with these mind-numbing, feeling-avoiding, and thought-silencing activities once you are alleviated of your unprocessed memories. You might start having real connections with people.

In some zombie movies, the zombie can run or move fast. Are you one of these kinds of zombies? The type that jog, or are committed to going to the gym, or are always busy doing anything and everything. There is nothing wrong with working out. It is essential to take care of yourself and be as fit and healthy as you can be.

My concern is the why behind what you do. You stay so busy doing this or that; you don't have time to think about how you feel. Are you one of those people who volunteer for everything and the only time you stop is when you become so sick you cannot get out of bed? Don't say no. I wrote "so sick you cannot get out of bed" because you are the kind of person that even though you are sick, you go to school, you go to practice, you go to work, you are at every church event or every help the world event, but the only one you never help is you!

Again, I believe in helping others. I practice giving back. I condone saving the world. I support being a productive member of society. The issue is not what you do, but why you do or don't do what you do. I love music, movies, some TV and playing games on the Wii or Xbox and technology but my point is, are you using this as a way to cope in the same way someone else would use prescription drugs, or illegal drugs or alcohol or sex or buying things or collecting things or a need for control? Everyone has their triggers, and everyone has their way of how they hold on by a string. This living at the edge of complete annihilation is NOT thriving.

Sometimes when you are sick, all you want to do is sleep. Sleep allows your body to heal itself. Well, memories have been locked away as a protection to enable you not to be overwhelmed by them which would cause you to shut down. Your mind has suppressed the memories, but your body is still responding to the pain of the abuse or the trauma.

What we think affects how we act and feel. You rationalize the thoughts when that does not help. You try to replace the feelings those thoughts bring up by activity, but eventually you get tired, and your defenses come down, and all those feelings rush back. What we feel, affects how we think and what we do. Some people resort to dulling the awareness of these feelings by alcohol and drugs, but eventually, your body resists that also. What we do affects how we think and feel. Use your energy wisely.

Why is your body fighting you? It is sending off alarms like an alarm in your house or car warning you that your life, joy, happiness, and peace are being confiscated. You must act, not react. We find ourselves talking about it, arguing about it, dreaming about it but no relief comes. It feels like the event is happening now, but it has been over. The area we are missing dealing with, is the loss of trust, loss of safety, loss of a say so about what happens to our property (your body, your emotions, your mind, and your spirit). Until you express and feel the loss that those events have caused, you will keep living it in the present.

Some of you may say, "I do feel it almost non-stop or every day." What you are feeling is a hose that has a knot in it. The water is on, the pressure is building, but the knot keeps you from feeling free-flowing emotions or relief. You must act to unblock the water pressure so that your feelings will flow. It is like a clog in your drain, everything sits there, rotting and smelling until the clog is relieved. This old memory is tainting your current experiences, stinking up your romance, blissfulness, and serenity. Sometimes, you have to dig the hair out of the sink to relieve the clog. Therapy is the digging; after a while you do not even know all that stuff that fell down the drain through the years that are clogging it.

Remember when you broke your leg, arm, finger, did your doctor just put a cast on it? No, he had to cause you pain to put the bone back in place. You had to take months to give yourself nurturing and healing care. If you did not follow the doctor's guidelines, you were right back at the doctor's office and the recovery time was extended. That is what you are going through now. You broke your toe, and you are letting it grow all messed up, but since it is your small toe, it is hidden in your shoe, so no one notices it. People see you are limping, but they say to themselves, "Maybe that is the way she ordinally walks because come to think of it, I never seen her walk without that limp."

It is time for you to learn how to care for yourself properly. Unlearn those unhelpful ways, that keep you stuck. Learn to love yourself by healing from your past, so you can get out of your fog, and see danger coming so you can avoid it. Without actively working on recovery, a person keeps attracting the old patterns that keep them believing the world is unsafe and people are vile.

We are avoiding the good because it is unfamiliar and thus scary. We return to what we know, controlling people or boundaryless people. If we keep running away from what we are afraid of, what we are so scared of only gets bigger. If we focus on healing and don't quit, we get what we put our energy on – HEALED!

Procrastination equals lethargy and paralysis. The negative thinking is re-enforced by suspicion, anxiety, and most likely you are surrounded by other people who feel and think like you. You might need to make some new friends and spend less time with particular family members that display traits fear and distrust. Redirect the constant negative and not productive thoughts, attitudes, and conversations for a while, making a conscious effort to replace them with what you want instead of what you don't want. For example, when we feel things are going well, we tend to brace ourselves waiting for the bottom to fall out thus missing out on the good that is happening right then and there. We don't trust the situation or the person's motives and, therefore, eventually, we burn the person out with our reservations, and sarcasm.

We turn the good guy/girl into the bad guy/girl in our minds, but we are just projecting the old story onto the new person. Instead of seeing life with rose-colored glasses, we see life through mud and gunk. To remove the muck, we have to notice our patterns. We have been doing it so long we forget why we started doing it and just accepted the behavior like it is who we are.

We are beautiful, loving, nurturing, funny, sensitive beings but the fear makes us have sharp edges. Think of yourself as a rose, you are lovely, brilliant in many colors, soft to the touch but the thorns stop people from holding you and taking you home. Therapy is your de-thorning. Don't let fear keep you immobilized. I know some of you may have wariness about exploring such painful memories. You may think, "I am going to open up this can of worms, and the floodgate of pain and tears are going to come bursting out, and I don't know how to turn it off." Or you may feel you barely lived through the pain the first time. Why would you ever return to it again? It is important to recognize this as negative thinking, but know that your thoughts can be transformed. This negative thinking is the exact pattern we are trying to terminate. The risk you would be taking by exploring your assumptions from the past will be worth it, once healed. Even though you try to avoid the pain of your past, you have not escaped it; there are things in your life that bring back the memory whether you like it or not. The old beliefs surrounding your trauma is what is causing damage, and it needs to be reprocessed so that

126

it gets filed away unable to pop up regularly causing you pain.

When you lose a pet or a friend or family member to death, you must mourn them. It takes times, and it is acceptable to mourn the loss. You are mourning the loss of your happy childhood, or your safety, or your virginity, or all of what your marriage represented to you that you lose when you got divorced or the things that fear and shame have taken from you. It is natural to feel pain, sorrow, unrelenting annoyance, and many other feelings because of not being protected, being neglected, ignored, devalued, used, abused, violated and controlled. You are no longer going to merely survive these tragic events because that is scraping by in life. You will THRIVE and BE ALIVE. YOU WILL BE HAPPY AND HAVE PEACE. DECLARE IT TO THE WORLD. IT IS YOUR RIGHT!

Remember with your new-found power do not become that which you hated or that hurt you. We have stayed passive so long it will be normal to swing the pendulum to the other extreme. Balance is our goal. Do not become the villain. You need to learn to embrace your emotions, feelings, trust yourself and finally be free! Just the fact that you do not feel your zeal or tenderness entirely equates that at least half of your responses to people are going to be hurtful to them. Why? Because your emotions lack depth, compassion, a soft heart, and are governed by fear. Fear is volatile and unpredictable.

Sometimes, the people who hurt us the most are abusive parents or spouses or people in the church. I use this scripture to remind me that what "they" call love is not.

"So, no matter what I say, what I believe, and what I do, I'm bankrupt without love.
Love never gives up. (Not an enabler)
Love cares more for others than for self (Not selfish, not codependent).
Love doesn't want what it doesn't have. (Not controlling or bully or thief)
Love doesn't strut (Not arrogant or a bully),
Doesn't have a swelled head, (Not prideful)
Doesn't force itself on others (Not a molester or rapist),
Isn't always "me first, (Not a robber, mugger, or embezzler, molester & rapist, or violent)"
Doesn't fly off the handle (Doesn't have anger issues, emotionally unstable but if they do, they get help on their own)
Doesn't keep score of the sins of others (Not a revenge seeker, self-righteous & unforgiving),
Doesn't revel when others grovel, (Not a Predator)
Doesn't takes pleasure in the flowering of truth (Not a pathological liar, white lies, half-truths),
Puts up with anything (Not actions that are abusive or illegal),
Trusts God always, (Won't do bad things in the shadows because they know God is watching)
Always looks for the best (Trusts and brings out the best in others by example),
Never looks back (Not stuck in the past good or bad),

But keeps going to the end (Strives)." 1 Corinthians 13:3-7 The Message (MSG)

"Real wisdom, God's wisdom, begins with a holy life and is characterized **by getting along with others. It is gentle and reasonable, overflowing with mercy** and blessings, **not hot one day and cold the next, not two-faced**. You can develop a healthy, robust community that lives right with God and enjoy its results only if you do the hard work of getting along with each other, **treating each other with dignity and honor.**" James 3:17-18 The Message (MSG)

Did that sound like your family or your marriage or your friendships? You can keep with the dysfunction - unstable, volatile, backstabbing and not to be trusted lifestyle or you can choose to move into the unfamiliar healthy world of healing.

When people are abusing you to make you submit that is not God's way, nor is it loving and you do not have to settle for that kind of life or treatment not even verbal abuse. If you grew up in a military family and your parents used shame, yelling, intimidation and control to get you to obey that is not discipline, it was emotional and maybe physical abuse.

Just because the military gets adults to follow the rules this way does not mean that this is the proper way to raise a kid or treat a spouse. The Armed Forces or terrorist groups use torture to get the truth out of people. Or do they? Do they just get people to say whatever they want to stop their suffering? Do you think this would be a good practice to incorporate in our school system just because it works sometimes?

You deserve better, by enforcing consequences like going to the authorities or to someone who can protect you and help you to remove yourself from the situation and to keep you safe. You will need someone who will walk you through getting restraining orders or filing a police report or going to the leaders of the church or school system - whoever is in charge of that residence, church, corporation or bar where the offense occurred.

"But **the one who always listens to me will live undisturbed in a heavenly peace. Free from fear, confident and courageous, you will rest unafraid and sheltered from the storms of life.**" Proverbs 1:33 The Passion Translation (TPT)

Forms of Therapy

A revolutionary new therapy called **EMDR** (Eye Movement Desensitization Reprocessing) created by Francine Shapiro gives relief to patients who suffer for years from anxiety or distressing memories, nightmares, insomnia, abuse or other traumatic events. EMDR is a powerful short-term therapy that is highly effective for chronic pain, phobias, depression, panic attacks, eating disorders and poor self-image, stress, worry, stage fright, performance anxiety, phobias, recovery from sexual abuse and traumatic incidents.

EMDR-Therapy will help for rape recovery, psychological abuse or neglect, abandonment experiences, marital betrayals, painful divorces, excessive anger, stress management, personal & spiritual growth, for adults emotionally, physically or sexually abused as children, PTSD - Post-traumatic stress disorder, and bring about rapid relief for shyness - fear of social situations, fear of public speaking, fear of heights, and the fear of the dentist. This treatment also works for overcoming low self-esteem, and self-limiting beliefs, performance blocks such as premature ejaculation, impotence, unable to reach orgasm, loss of sexual desire or sexual and intimacy enrichment.

Neuro Emotional Technique (NET) was created in the 1980s by Scott Walker. "NET Practitioners are nearly unlimited in their ability to address the physical and behavioral stress-related conditions of their patients. These conditions include headaches, body pains, phobias, general anxiety, self-sabotaging behaviors, organ dysfunctions and so much more. NET removes blocks to the essential vitals of the body, "allowing" the body to repair itself naturally. In many cases, a Pulse Correction and a Spinal Correction is used, and once the correction is made, the body's unresolved stress patterns can start to move toward the desired direction of homeostasis and balance.

Certified NET Mind-Oriented Practitioners are trained to use The Home Run Formula model, with 1st base representing emotional/stress-related factors, 2nd base representing the effects of toxins on the body, 3rd base deals with nutritional needs, and 4th base addresses structural needs.

Gary Craig created **Emotional Freedom Technique (EFT)** as an alternative treatment for physical pain and emotional distress. "It's also referred to as tapping or psychological acupressure." EFT tapping has been used to treat people with anxiety

131

and people with post-traumatic stress disorder (PTSD). EFT uses fingertip tapping to apply pressure to meridian points just like acupuncture uses needles to help balance energy flow to maintain your health. Imbalances can influence disease or sickness. There are seven tapping spots - the eyebrow, side of the eye, under the eye, under the nose, chin, the collarbone and under the arm. You need to establish a phrase that explains what you're trying to address. "It must focus on two main goals; acknowledging the issues and accepting yourself despite the problem. The common setup phrase is: "Even though I have this [fear or problem], I deeply and completely accept myself."

Grief Recovery is an action program that is not just for loss from death but the loss of many common issues in life including divorce, career, health, faith, trauma, and PTSD. John W. James and Russell Friedman are the Founders of The Grief Recovery Institute and authors as well. I highly recommend "The Grief Recovery Handbook" because it helps you work through many issues regarding starting school, graduation, financial changes, empty nest, end of addictions, moving, and the holidays which is one of the major suicide periods in the world.

It only needs three things to work - you, 'The Grief Recovery" book and one positive and good listening safe person (GR specialist). It includes letter writing and timelines called a "History Graph" or "Relationship Graph" of significant events. You will be journaling. The main categories are on comments people said that were not helpful and the beliefs you took on from others that were not constructive. There are three other writing categories: apologies, forgiveness, and significant emotional statements. There are some key phrases that they use that are more powerful than you would ever think. For example, "I need to forgive you .... so that I can be free." The apology section relieves guilt, and the significant emotional statement expresses how what you forgave them for made you feel. It works!

It teaches you about labels like "survivor" which often becomes an identity with pain and it causes you to revisit the circumstance of that pain continually. This word has now become a definition and a diagnosis that keeps people stuck. I suggest you go to a Grief Recovery Specialist to complete one significant event in your life, so you know how it works. Then you can work the other issues up to a certain point and then go in for another visit so you can read your correspondence letter to the GR Specialist. Three steps must be done to help you create your letter which is the final step in the process. This is where you will need help from the GR Specialist. There are some dead-end phrases that the specialists will identify and help you rephrase. This program fixes whatever is incomplete so that you can move forward.

Another option to get assistance for issues that you may have is **Group Therapy** which is meeting with a group of people going through relatable life challenges with a therapist there to guide the group with specific topics. Most **psychotherapies** are facilitated with a licensed and trained mental health care professional and a patient meeting one on one or with other patients in a group setting. The people in the specific groups could be dealing with severe or long-term stress from a job or family situation, the loss of a loved one, or relationship or other family issues. Or they may be there because they have symptoms with no physical explanation: changes in sleep or appetite, low energy, a lack of interest or pleasure in activities that they once enjoyed, persistent irritability, or a sense of discouragement or hopelessness that won't go away. They may have been diagnosed with any of these conditions such as depression, bipolar disorder, post-traumatic stress or other disorders and recommended psychotherapy as a first treatment or to go along with medication.

Sigmund Freud created **Psychoanalysis and psychodynamic therapies**, but it has been extended and modified since his early methods. **One on One Therapy** is centered around changing problematic behaviors, feelings, and thoughts by discovering their unconscious meanings and motivations. Psychoanalytical therapies are a close working partnership between therapist and patient. Patients learn about themselves.

Humanistic therapy was created by Humanistic philosophers Jean-Paul Sartre, Soren Kierkegaard, and Martin Buber emphasizes people's capacity to make rational choices and develop to their maximum potential while showing concern and respect for the client. Three types of humanistic therapy are **Client-centered therapy, Gestalt therapy, and Existential therapy. Client-centered therapy** rebels against the traditional idea of therapists as authorities on their clients' internal experiences. Their approach is the therapists help clients change by emphasizing their concern, care, and interest. **Gestalt therapy** emphasizes what it calls "organismic holism," the importance of being aware of the here and now and accepting responsibility for yourself. Eckhart Etolle, the author of "The Power of Now" explains this concept very well. **Existential therapy** emphasizes free will, self-determination and the search for meaning. **Integrative or holistic therapy** combines elements from different approaches and acclimates their treatment according to each client's needs.

Behavior therapy is an approach that focuses on learning roles in developing both normal and abnormal behaviors. You may be familiar with the experiment performed by Ivan Pavlov's famous dogs, who began drooling when they heard their dinner bell because they associated the sound with food. Pavlov made essential strides in behavior therapy by discovering **classical conditioning**, or associative learning. The behavior therapy called **Desensitizing** is classical conditioning in action; a therapist might help a client with a phobia through repeated exposure to whatever it is that causes anxiety.

I practiced Desensitizing before I knew it was a therapy. I used to be terrified of rodents. I tried desensitizing myself by studying every kind of rodent. The result was my list of what I was afraid of was growing. Then I started digging to find out why I was frightened of these creatures; once I discovered it, and processed the thinking behind it in a healthy way, that is when the fear went away. I can now see them on movies and TV or posters with no reaction where before I would scream and turn away.

Then I tried desensitizing myself with childhood movies that caused me to fret. I sat and watched the film with my husband whom I trusted and who would not get up and leave or try to scare me during the movie or make a joke of it. Someone belittling you or making you feel foolish for having fear is not helpful. If your reactions are severe, I would recommend working with a professional. This method helped me to get over my nightmares about these movies.

I remember the first movie I watched during this desensitization process; I was tense the whole time, waiting to be scared and then the movie was over. I realized my mind magnified the entire film, and I dreamed about it because my mind was trying to create an ending to that which I heard about but had never seen. This event is why I suggest not exposing young kids to inappropriate programs; their brains are not mature enough to handle it, and it can become a trauma. Once I saw Aliens (the movie), I never dreamed about it again. Our minds are continually trying to problem solve; if you work with it, instead of running from it, your healing will be achieved sooner.

E. L. Thorndike discovered **Operant Conditioning** which is a type of learning that relies on rewards and punishments to shape people's behavior. **Cognitive-behavioral therapy** is one of the treatments in the operant conditioning which focuses on both thoughts and conduct. Cognitive therapy focuses on what people think rather than what they do. The more well-known Cognitive therapists are Albert Ellis and

Aaron Beck that believe it is dysfunctional thinking that leads to dysfunctional emotions or behaviors. By changing their thoughts, people can change how they feel and what they do.

I have found exploring what I think is very valuable because sometimes you believe things that are inherited from a family member or our culture that once you think about it, you realize it is not accurate. Without exploring the information that we are hearing; what we believe, feel or act on, once examined, we may find out that what we presume is the exception, not the rule which without exploration, we can assume it is a highly probable occurrence.

"A Message from the high and towering God, who lives in Eternity, whose name is Holy: "**I live in the high and holy places, but also with the low-spirited, the spirit-crushed, and what I do is put a new spirit in them, get them up and on their feet again.**" Isaiah 57:14-15 The Message (MSG)

CHAPTER SEVEN

NEW LIFE

I recommend that you journal. Write down your feelings. You will discover one day when you go back to read it; you will be amazed at how far you have come.

As a kid, I had many diaries. Once I was an adult, I went back to read those diaries. It is incredible how our viewpoint changes, how what we thought was normal was so dysfunctional or immature, sometimes. Our prefrontal cortex does not fully develop until we are 25 years old. When we experience trauma, we get stuck at the age the situation occurred. We grow older, yet emotionally we could be age 5, 12, 18, or 23 years old, depending on when the event transpired. You have seen people who are in their forties but still wearing a backpack everywhere like a high school student or wearing clothes that a college student would be wearing. Their wardrobe is most likely because they are stuck, not because they like that style. I am sure you have known relatives or acquaintances that are very irresponsible with finances or still playing the field like some teenager going through puberty - very driven by impulse and pleasure seeking. Trying different therapies will help a person mature emotionally and mentally. Our viewpoint about certain things needs to be rejuvenated.

Let us take the time to write out what you want; consider this is your wish list, nothing is too big or too small of a statement.

I will provide some examples. Do not phrase these as "I want" or "need." The word "want" shows it is lacking, and you want to state it as if you have it now. If you phrase it as "tomorrow," it will always be a day away. Tomorrow never comes; it is always today or now. I like to create a Thank You List because it generates positive feelings. You can write a Grateful List of what you already have, then write what you want to have as "Thank you for...." Remember never write down what "you don't want." Your words and thoughts create your future. God spoke things into existence, and we are made in his image. See the scripture below to validate this.

"And God said, "Let there be light," and there was light." Genesis 1:3 New International Version (NIV)

"With the tongue, we praise our Lord and Father, and with it, we curse **human beings, who have been made in God's likeness.**" James 3:9 New International Version (NIV)

"This is the written account of Adam's family line. **When God created mankind, he made them in the likeness of God.**" Genesis 5:1 New International Version (NIV)

Try to feel what it would feel like to have what you are desiring - like being healthier, more fit, really supported by your family or fulfilled in your career. You should practice saying this in your head when you have doubts, or negative thoughts emerge. I would write the repeating doubts, in an opposite phrase and look at it often. For example, if you call yourself "stupid" when you make a mistake, create the phrase, "I learn from my mistakes, and I am smarter because of it." I would say it in front of a mirror with a smile of confidence, this is your propaganda.

Remember once you start learning what a safe person looks like, you may find that you have some unsafe tendencies. Do not fear or beat yourself up. Embrace who you are and be willing to change. No one is perfect including you or your new safe friends. Do not isolate. Give grace to yourself and others. Remember, if any of these things on the list below don't apply, you can focus on that which does apply.

We can become enablers because it makes us feel worthy or we feel good about ourselves, but it is destructive. People become our projects. We need to start to repair ourselves first.

There was always one person at my job that would make it a challenging work environment but 99% of the other people were kind, helpful, positive, friendly, and fun. I had to learn to refocus my energy. It helped me to be grateful because we don't live in a perfect world. We can choose to focus on the problems or the blessings. It is up to us. We control our thoughts and our feelings. When we are grateful for what we have we open up our life for more opportunities to be appreciative.

Grateful List

I AM GRATEFUL TO BE ALIVE!
I AM GRATEFUL TO BE HEALTHY!
I AM GRATEFUL TO BE A PARENT!
I AM GRATEFUL TO BE A SPOUSE!
I AM GRATEFUL TO HAVE FRIENDS WITH GOOD BOUNDARIES!

I AM GRATEFUL TO HAVE A JOB THAT I LOVE!

I AM GRATEFUL TO HAVE A JOB THAT RESPECTS AND VALUES ME!

I AM GRATEFUL TO BE ABLE TO TRAVEL!

I AM GRATEFUL TO HAVE A JOB THAT PAYS ME WELL!

I AM GRATEFUL TO LIVE IN (STATE, COUNTRY)!

I AM GRATEFUL TO HAVE FOUND FAMILY THAT LOVES ME UNCONDITIONALLY!

I AM GRATEFUL TO HAVE_____ THAT SHOWED ME, UNCONDITIONAL LOVE!

I AM GRATEFUL FOR _____ MY FAVORITE TEACHER/COACH!

I AM GRATEFUL FOR _____ MY FAVORITE FOOD!

I AM GRATEFUL FOR SUCH A VARIETY OF DELICIOUS FOODS!

I AM GRATEFUL TO HAVE CLOTHES TO WEAR!

I AM GRATEFUL TO HAVE A COMFORTABLE HOME!

I AM GRATEFUL FOR MY BEST FRIEND _____!

I AM GRATEFUL TO HAVE FOUND MY PURPOSE IN LIFE!

I AM GRATEFUL TO KNOW THAT MY CREATOR LOVES ME UNCONDITIONALLY!

I AM GRATEFUL FOR GRACE AND FORGIVENESS!

Thankful List

I AM THANKFUL FOR REALIZING I AM WORTH LOVING!

I AM THANKFUL THAT I LOVE MYSELF AND ACCEPT MYSELF!

I AM THANKFUL THAT I AM HAPPY AND I DESERVE HAPPINESS AND PEACE IN MY LIFE!

I AM THANKFUL TO HAVE COURAGE!

I AM THANKFUL TO BE SAFE!

I AM THANKFUL THAT I RESPECT MYSELF AND EXPECT OTHERS TO RESPECT ME!

I AM THANKFUL THAT I AM UNCONDITIONALLY LOVED BY ALL WHO ARE CLOSE TO ME!

I AM THANKFUL I AM WORTH MORE THAN I EVER IMAGINED AND NOW I KNOW IT!

I AM THANKFUL THAT I ACCEPT MYSELF UNCONDITIONALLY!

I AM THANKFUL I SLEEP SOUNDLY AND PEACEFULLY!

I AM THANKFUL I AM IN CONTROL OF MY LIFE, AND I HAVE TAKEN MY POWER BACK!

I AM GRATEFUL TO HAVE GOOD/ EXCELLENT CREDIT!

I AM THANKFUL FOR ALL THE WAYS I LOVE MYSELF!

I AM THANKFUL I CAN BE MYSELF AROUND MY FRIENDS AND FAMILY!

I AM THANKFUL I AM THRIVING!

I AM THANKFUL I AM CAPABLE!

I AM THANKFUL MY RELATIONSHIPS ARE GETTING MORE POSITIVE AND HEALTHIER EVERY DAY!

I AM THANKFUL THAT I CAN LET GO OF THE THOUGHTS THAT DO NOT SERVE ME!

I AM THANKFUL I AM FULL OF POSITIVE ENERGY!

I AM THANKFUL I AM LEARNING WHO THE SAFE PEOPLE ARE!

I AM THANKFUL MY BODY CAN HEAL ITSELF, AND I WILL DO WHATEVER IS WITHIN MY POWER TO AID IT WITH GOOD NUTRITION, EXERCISE, 8 HOURS OF SLEEP AND WATER CONSUMPTION!

I ACCEPT AND LOVE MY BODY JUST THE WAY IT IS, AT THE SAME TIME MOVING TOWARDS HEALTH!

I AM THANKFUL TO BE GROWING IN MY KNOWLEDGE ABOUT EMOTIONAL, PHYSICAL AND SPIRITUAL HEALTH!

I AM THANKFUL TO BE ABLE TO SEE MY LIFE GETTING BETTER AND BETTER!

I AM THANKFUL MY LIFE HAS SURPASSED MY HIGHEST HOPES AND DREAMS!

I AM THANKFUL I ENJOY MY FOOD AND EAT IN NORMAL PORTIONS!

I AM HAPPY WHEN I AM EATING AND AFTER I EAT!

I AM THANKFUL I CAN TREAT MYSELF TO A DESSERT, JUNK FOOD EVERY NOW AND THEN WITHOUT GUILT!

I AM THANKFUL FOR PEACE IN MY MIND AND IN MY LIFE!

I CAN BE ANYTHING I SET MY MIND TO ACHIEVE, AND I AM THANKFUL FOR IT!

I AM THANKFUL TO HAVE A GREAT SUPPORT SYSTEM!

I AM THANKFUL I STARTED AND COMPLETED THIS JOURNEY OF HEALING AND THAT I RECOGNIZE MY TRIGGERS AND THEY ARE REPROCESSED AND VANISHING!

I AM THANKFUL MY PAST IS IN THE PAST. I CAN NOW USE MY PAST TO HELP OTHERS!

I AM THANKFUL THAT I ENJOY DATING AND HAVE LONGER RELATIONSHIPS THAN EVER BEFORE!

I AM THANKFUL MY SPOUSE TREATS ME AS A RESPECTED PARTNER AND FRIEND!

I AM THANKFUL I CAN SAY "NO" AND FEEL OK WITH IT WITHOUT LONG EXPLANATIONS!

I AM THANKFUL THAT ANY NEW THING THAT POPS UP FROM MY PAST THAT I NEED TO WORK ON IS JUST CLEARING THE WAY FOR AN AWESOME FUTURE FOR ME!

I AM THANKFUL FOR SECURITY WITHIN MYSELF!

I AM THANKFUL THAT I AM OK WITH BEING ALONE!

I AM THANKFUL FOR THE PEOPLE IN MY LIFE THAT ENCOURAGE ME!

I AM THANKFUL TO BE GOOD ENOUGH. I AM ALWAYS GROWING IN A POSITIVE DIRECTION!

I AM GRATEFUL THAT I HAVE PEOPLE THAT ARE TRUSTWORTHY!

I AM THANKFUL THAT I HAVE PEOPLE WHO TELL ME THE TRUTH IN A LOVING WAY!

I LOVE THAT I CAN ACCEPT A COMPLIMENT, AND I AM THANKFUL FOR BEING WORTHY OF THESE COMPLIMENTS!

I AM THANKFUL I HAVE BROKEN MY OLD NEGATIVE PATTERNS, AND MY NEW HABITS ARE BENEFICIAL AND REWARDING!

I AM THANKFUL I MAKE LOVE WHEN I WANT TO, AND IT IS VERY SATISFYING!

I AM THANKFUL THAT I MATTER IN THIS WORLD!

I AM THANKFUL THAT I DON'T HAVE TO AVOID ANYTHING ANY MORE!

I AM THANKFUL THAT I AM IN TOUCH WITH ALL MY RANGE OF EMOTIONS!

I LOVE WHEN MY SOUL-MATE AND I CUDDLE AND I AM THANKFUL FOR THAT!

I AM THANKFUL I CAN WATCH OR READ THE NEWS, WATCH TV OR A MOVIE WITHOUT BEING IMMOBILIZED! ANY NEW TRIGGERS THAT SHOW THEMSELVES, I DEAL WITH THEM RIGHT AWAY!

I AM THANKFUL THAT I CAN FORGIVE MYSELF AND OTHERS BECAUSE IT FREES ME UP TO MOVE IN A POSITIVE DIRECTION IN MY PRESENT AND FUTURE!

I AM THANKFUL TO BE ABLE TO LEARN FROM THE PAST. IT WAS NOT MY FAULT. I TAKE RESPONSIBILITY FOR MY BELIEFS ABOUT MYSELF DUE TO THE EVENTS OF MY PAST, AND I HAVE THE POWER TO CHANGE MY BELIEFS!

Remember you are unique. No one, even if other people were hurt in the same way as you were, no one feels precisely the way you do or reacts the way you do. Nothing is wrong with how you handled your grief or trauma; you survived, and now you are heading on a path to let go of the unhealthy practices regarding how you dealt with your pain. Everything you feel will not match with someone else's feelings or experience. You must not compare or belittle what happened to you just because you think someone else's situation was more tragic than yours. What you went through affected you and that is what makes it matter because you are one of a kind; you have a purpose here, and you are needed.

Consider the people who had the most difficult lives, challenging experiences and unthinkable acts carried out against them and survived, these people are the ones who turn that pain around and end up helping many people. Even if you help only yourself, your kids or your friends, so the next generation is Thrivers not only survivors, it would be worth going through this journey of healing. I have faith in you!

"If you've gotten anything at all out of following Christ, if his love has made any difference in your life, if being in a community of the Spirit means anything to you, if you have a heart, if you *care* - then do me a favor: Agree with each other, **love each other, be deep-spirited friends.**" Philippians 2:1 The Message (MSG)

The scripture above tells us we were meant to love and have deep friendships. Our past traumas make it hard to know how to obtain this safe and healthy love and friendship. I recommend reading "Safe People" by Dr. Henry Cloud and Dr. Robert Townsend because most of us with abuse in our past consider dysfunction as normal; this book tells us what normal should look like.

No matter what stage in life you are in, one of these books mentioned below will help change a relationship to safe or help you recognize a safe way to retreat from that relationship if it is dangerous. Keep in mind, we learn by observing what we see as we mature so our kids will, more often than not, continue the bad or good pattern, we have displayed whether we speak against it or not. We only know what we are exposed to everything else seems non-existent or a fantasy. These books enable you to build a foundation for your present or future children to have a better start in life by helping you learn boundaries, teaching them boundaries and choosing a partner that have boundaries. The books are "Boundaries," "Boundaries with Kids," "Boundaries with Teens," "Boundaries in Dating," or "Boundaries in Marriage" by Dr. Henry Cloud and Dr. Robert Townsend. If you are a slow reader, you can choose an audiobook. If you don't like anyone to see what you are reading by buying a paperback book, buy an e-book.

Charge into this healing like you would when the Black Friday store doors open! Do not stop until you have achieved your desired wishes. I believe in you! I will be sending out positive thoughts and prayers for your healing. Those who have a negative body image about themselves should get the audiobook by Louise L. Hay called "Love Your Body; it is positive affirmations for loving and appreciating your body." I say audiobook because you can play it before you go to sleep or when you feel negativity, and it works on your subconscious to erase any negative statements people have said to you in the past or present or that you have said to yourself. Another excellent book for self-esteem is by Louise L. Hay called "Self-esteem Affirmations" that are both audible and subliminal.

When I did not know how to love myself unconditionally, I read about how God and Jesus loved me and said they created everything and since I am precious to Beings that are so important, I had to start allowing myself to feel it. If males like David and Jonathan can have unconditional love and are able to express their deep friendship with one another, why should a female (the leader in showing emotions and communication) be afraid to make full use of her heart?

"Jonathan was deeply impressed with David - an immediate bond was forged between them. He became totally committed to David. From that point on he would be David's number-one advocate and friend." 1 Samuel 18:1 The Message (MSG)

"Jonathan, out of his deep love for David, made a covenant with him. He formalized it with solemn gifts: his own royal robe and weapons - armor, sword, bow, and belt." 1 Samuel 18:3-4 The Message (MSG)

Remember, we helped create this world in our own way. We women, birthed the Presidents of the USA, The Queens, and Kings of the UK, the Presidents and CEOs of Google, Amazon, Facebook, etc. We peopled this world with everyone that makes this world thrive. We have a purpose! We loved and nurtured those people who are brave enough to get in front of a camera and report the news or sing on stage or to perform a play or cook delicious meals as Head Chef for the millionaires and billionaires of this world! We birthed those teachers that help the whole world succeed. We fed those boys and girls healthy meals and drove them to practice so they could win gold, silver, and bronze in the Olympics or win the championship in sports. We need each other to succeed. Without men, we would not be able to create children, so we need each other. We need to work as a team for this world to succeed.

A man should not be ashamed to report he was harmed in anyway. He has a right to feel safe and be safe. Rape or molestation is a crime just like mugging or murder. If you don't get the help you need to be whole; it hurts society. Anger, fear, distrust, depression, and suicides will overtake this world in a matter of years. Healing the world starts with each person making a stand for their own mental, emotional and physical health.

Think of who you would like to be or what you would want to do to help motivate you to finish the healing process. Think what a better lover, friend, employee, or leader you will be once you are revitalized.

If the Messiah is not afraid to cry, why should we be fearful that our emotions will overtake us? He felt everything everyone he ever created experienced. That is a perfect example of overcoming the past! The universe's Creator values facing fears, and disappointments. Remember Jesus was betrayed, abandoned, assaulted physically and verbally, bullied, and humiliated. He works through these issues with scriptures and prayer. Why wouldn't it work for everyone else?

"While he lived on earth, anticipating death, **Jesus cried out in pain and wept in sorrow** as **he offered** up priestly **prayers to God**." Hebrews 5:7 The Message (MSG)

Facing the truth brings healing. The loss is real, and everyone goes through at least one unfortunate crisis in their life; the sooner we know the proper way to deal with it, the more successful we will be. You are not alone.

"I'll be with you as you do this, **day after day after day, right up to the end of the age**." Matthew 28:20 The Message (MSG)

"Then, by constantly using your faith, the life of Christ will be released deep inside you, and the resting place of his love will become the very source and root of your life. **Then you will be empowered** to discover what every holy one experiences - **the great**

magnitude of the astonishing love of Christ in all its dimensions. How deeply intimate and far-reaching is his love! How enduring and inclusive it is! Endless love beyond measurement that transcends our understanding - this extravagant love pours into you until you are filled to overflowing with the fullness of God!" Ephesians 3:17-19 The Passion Translation (TPT)

This love from God is not exclusive; you don't have to be wealthy, perfect, beautiful, talented, a male or be in a particular club or be a specific skin color. You are accepted just because you want it. No matter what you achieve in life, there will be a feeling something is missing because that space is meant for receiving your Creator's love and having a personal relationship with them (God, Jesus, and the Holy Spirit). I am not pushing religion. I am saying we are spiritual beings and we need to feed our spirit. Life is not about traditions and rules, it is about love, family, relationships, community, caring, helping, feeling, sharing, and bonding, being able to express hope, and passion, through your gifts and talents and just being a part of something that matters to you.

"He has made everything beautiful and appropriate in its time. **He has also planted eternity [a sense of divine purpose] in the human heart [a mysterious longing which nothing under the sun can satisfy, except God]** - yet man cannot find out (comprehend, grasp) what God has done (His overall plan) from the beginning to the end." Ecclesiastes 3:11 AMP

SOURCES

1. National Institute of Justice & Centers for Disease Control & Prevention, Prevalence, Incidence, and Consequences of Violence Against Women Survey (1998).
2. Department of Justice, Office of Justice Programs, Bureau of Justice Statistics, National Crime Victimization Survey, 2012-2016 (2017).
3. David Cantor, Bonnie Fisher, Susan Chibnall, Reanna Townsend, et. al. Association of American Universities (AAU), Report on the AAU Campus Climate Survey on Sexual Assault and Sexual Misconduct (September 21, 2015).
4. RAINN (Rape, Abuse & Incest National Network).
5. Department of Justice, Office of Justice Programs, Bureau of Justice Statistics, American Indians and Crime, 1992-2002 (2004).
6. D.S. Riggs, T. Murdock, W. Walsh, A prospective examination of post-traumatic stress disorder in rape victims. Journal of Traumatic Stress 455-475 (1992).
7. J. R. T. Davidson & E. B. Foa (Eds.) Posttraumatic Stress Disorder: DSM-IV and Beyond. American Psychiatric Press: Washington, DC. (pp. 23-36).

8. DG Kilpatrick, CN Edumuds, AK Seymour. Rape in America: A Report to the Nation. Arlington, VA: National Victim Center and Medical University of South Carolina (1992).
9. Department of Justice, Office of Justice Programs, Bureau of Justice Statistics, Socio-emotional Impact of Violent Crime (2014).

ABOUT THE AUTHOR

Jennifer Gamboa has three degrees in which she graduated Cum Laude (with honors) in Business Management. As a full-time working mother for a Fortune 500 company, she uses her free time to volunteer for many activities. She motives people to go after their dreams. Jennifer has an IQ of 136. She is the Co-Author of "You Deserve the Good Things in Life" which is in five countries. Jen loves to learn, and in the last three years has read over 138 non-fiction books, reading each one at least 2 to 5 times. She has read many different versions of the Scriptures from beginning to end and uses it to encourage and inspire others.

Mrs. Gamboa has overcome many challenges in her life. In the last twenty-one years, she has helped others heal from their past abuse, and handle with dignity marital and health problems. Jennifer has a Black Belt in Taekwondo and teaches special needs kids to protect themselves from ruffians. She has been called "The strongest person they know" by many people. She is a role model on how to stop barely surviving to someone who embraced THRIVING!

Printed in the United States
By Bookmasters